JOHNSON

Selections and Criticism

Oxford University Press, Ely House, London W. 1

GLASGOW NEW YORK TORONTO MELBOURNE WELLINGTON
CAPE TOWN SALISBURY IBADAN NAIROBI DAR ES SALAAM LUSAKA ADDIS ABABA
BOMBAY CALCUTTA MADRAS KARACHI LAHORE DACCA
KUALA LUMPUR SINGAPORE HONG KONG TOKYO

FIRST PUBLISHED 1922
REPRINTED 1925, 1927, 1934, 1938, 1943, 1949, 1953, 1956,
1961, 1964, 1970

PRINTED IN GREAT BRITAIN

SAMUEL JOHNSON

From the painting by Reynolds in the
National Portrait Gallery

JOHNSON

Prose & Poetry

With Boswell's Character

Macaulay's Life and

Raleigh's Essay

With an Introduction and Notes by

R. W. CHAPMAN

OXFORD

AT THE CLARENDON PRESS

CONTENTS

The Edition of Shakespeare—
  From the Preface :

A Journey to the Western Islands :

The Lives of the Poets—

OCCASIONAL WRITINGS and LETTERS—

INTRODUCTION

It has been claimed for the series of which this little book is a member, that its plan obviates to a large extent the tedious necessity of editorial introduction and explanation. An editor who is fortunate in his material, and judicious in his use of it, finds that his critical extracts explain each other, as they explain and are in turn explained by the selections with which they are combined. Having placed his field, he may stand aside and leave the game to the players.

An editor who approaches Johnson upon this plan is especially fortunate in both the quantity and the quality of the material from which he is to make his choice. From few writers is it less difficult to choose passages of great and characteristic excellence, which suffer but little by removal from their context. And good criticism of the man and of his works is not only abundant, but is in a high degree stimulating and entertaining.

Many good Johnsonians, I am afraid, will regard the inclusion of Macaulay's *Life* as a timid following of tradition. Macaulay's paradoxes, it will be said, were long since exploded, and it is now time they were forgotten. Yet I have ventured not only to print the *Life* in its entirety, but to print it without notes. For including it there are two good reasons : in the first place, nearly all later criticism of Johnson assumes a knowledge of Macaulay's views, and is concerned largely with their confutation ; in the second place, the *Life* is still the best short introduction to the subject.[1] It is incomparably brilliant and vivid ; it contains much that is true, and that could not be better stated. For leaving it without notes, again, I think I can plead a better reason than the obvious lack of

[1] It is much less intemperate, and more judicious, than the famous review of Croker's Boswell written twenty-five years earlier.

space. It is, indeed, packed with allusions, many of which will be imperfectly understood. But as Mr. Nichol Smith has remarked,[1] in his admirable edition, one of Macaulay's conspicuous excellences is that his allusions are so introduced as partly to explain themselves.

Macaulay's errors are more serious than his obscurities ; but here too I am happily spared the necessity of exposing them by any arguments of my own. His exaggerations, amounting often to gross perversions of the truth, all find their corrective within the pages of this volume ; either in the Johnsonian pieces themselves, or in the true and living portrait of his hero which I quote from Boswell, or in the luminous essay which Sir Walter Raleigh allows me to include as representative of his wise and

[1] ' Macaulay has the supreme faculty of making his allusions to a certain extent self-explanatory. We know from the context that the Queensberrys and Lepels were famous beauties, that Junius and Skinner were antiquated etymologists, that Mrs. Lennox and Mrs. Sheridan were accomplished authoresses, and that Almon and Stockdale were the chief retailers of the political pamphlets of the day.' Macaulay's *Life of Johnson*, edited by D. Nichol Smith ; Blackwood, 1900.

discriminating judgements alike of Johnson and of his critics. This book, accordingly, abounds in contradiction and diversity of opinion. The intelligent reader, I believe, will enjoy the war of wits, and will be well content to form his own opinions.[1]

In my selections from Johnson I have sought to choose such pieces as will give some idea of the quality and range of his verse and prose, and may perhaps tempt the reader to make excursions for himself into the wide and all but untrodden expanses of the Collected Works.

I begin with *The Vanity of Human Wishes*. Sir Walter Scott told James Ballantyne that ' neither his own nor any modern popular style of composition was that from which he derived most pleasure'. Ballantyne asked what it was ; ' He answered—Johnson's ; and that he had more pleasure in reading *London*, and *The Vanity of Human Wishes*, than any other poetical com-

---

[1] ' The mind is prompted to study and enquiry rather by the uneasiness of ignorance, than the hope of profit.'—*Rambler*, No. 161.

positions he could mention.'   Elsewhere Scott
wrote that ' the deep and pathetic morality of
the *Vanity of Human Wishes* has often extracted
tears from those whose eyes wander dry over
pages professedly sentimental'.   It seemed
right to print the *Vanity* in full.   The poem is
in some places obscure to those who come to it
with no great acquaintance with the poetry of
its age, and—as may well be—with no knowledge of its Latin original ; some annotation
therefore seemed necessary.   But the *Vanity*
is not a poem that can be read for the first time
with rapid ease ; it will not yield its meaning
or its beauty without close attention, and even
some effort, on the reader's part.   In such a case
even full notes may be useful, and perhaps need
no apology.

On the prose pieces I have found no occasion
to write many notes, except where Johnson's
criticism of other writers tempted me to go
beyond a mere mention of names and dates,
and to add some illustrative anecdotes and
quotations.   This book will have served its

purpose best if it persuades some of its readers
to the experiment of reading *Rasselas* and the
Journey to the Western Islands for pure amusement ; of dipping into the *Ramblers* in search
of wisdom rather than of pedantry ; or of
turning to the *Lives of the Poets* as to one of the
best of all guides to the enjoyment of literature
and the knowledge of life.

DATES

1752. The last *Rambler*, 14 March. Johnson's wife dies.

1755. Letter to Lord Chesterfield. Master of Arts of the University of Oxford.

    A Dictionary of the English Language, in which the Words are deduced from their Originals, and illustrated in their different Significations by Examples from the Best Writers : in two volumes folio.

1756. *Proposals for printing the Dramatick Works of William Shakespeare.*

1758–60. *The Idler* (15 April 1758—5 April 1760).

1759. His mother dies. *Rasselas, Prince of Abissinia.*

1760. Accession of George III.

1762. Receives from the Crown a pension of £300 a year. James Macpherson's *Fingal*, purporting to be a translation of the ancient Gaelic poetry of Ossian.

1763. Meets James Boswell, 16 May.

1764. Foundation of the Club, proposed by Sir (then Mr.) Joshua Reynolds, and later known as the Literary Club.

1765. His edition of Shakespeare.

    Bishop Percy's *Reliques of Ancient Poetry.*

1766. Goldsmith's *Vicar of Wakefield.*

1767. Has an interview with the King.

1771. *Thoughts on the late Transactions respecting Falkland's Islands.*

1773. Visits the Highlands and Islands with Boswell.

1774. Death of Goldsmith.

1775. *A Journey to the Western Islands of Scotland.*

    Made D.C.L. by the University of Oxford.

1779. *Prefaces, Biographical and Critical, to the Works of the English Poets*, Vols. 1–4.

1781. *Prefaces*, Vols. 5–10 ; also another edition of the whole, in four volumes, now called *Lives of the Most Eminent English Poets.*

1783. Revised edition of the *Lives.*

1784. Dies, 13 December, and is buried in Westminster Abbey.

THE

L I F E

OF

SAMUEL JOHNSON, LL.D.

COMPREHENDING

AN ACCOUNT OF HIS STUDIES

AND NUMEROUS WORKS,

IN CHRONOLOGICAL ORDER;

A SERIES OF HIS EPISTOLARY CORRESPONDENCE

AND CONVERSATIONS WITH MANY EMINENT PERSONS;

AND

VARIOUS ORIGINAL PIECES OF HIS COMPOSITION,

NEVER BEFORE PUBLISHED:

THE WHOLE EXHIBITING A VIEW OF LITERATURE AND
LITERARY MEN IN GREAT-BRITAIN, FOR NEAR
HALF A CENTURY, DURING WHICH HE
FLOURISHED.

By JAMES BOSWELL, Esq.

———— *Quò fit ut* OMNIS
Votiva pateat veluti descripta tabella
VITA SENIS. ————   HORAT.

THE THIRD EDITION, REVISED AND AUGMENTED,

IN FOUR VOLUMES.

VOLUME THE FIRST.

LONDON:

PRINTED BY H. BALDWIN AND SON,

FOR CHARLES DILLY, IN THE POULTRY.

MDCCXCIX.

From JAMES BOSWELL'S

LIFE OF SAMUEL JOHNSON, LL.D.

*First published in 1791 ; the extract follows the third edition
(the last revised by Boswell), 1799.*

THE character of SAMUEL JOHNSON has, I trust, been so
developed in the course of this work, that they who have
honoured it with a perusal, may be considered as well
acquainted with him. As, however, it may be expected
that I should collect into one view the capital and dis-
tinguishing features of this extraordinary man, I shall
endeavour to acquit myself of that part of my biographical
undertaking,[1] however difficult it may be to do that which
many of my readers will do better for themselves.

His figure was large and well formed, and his counte- 10
nance of the cast of an ancient statue ; yet his appearance
was rendered strange and somewhat uncouth, by con-
vulsive cramps, by the scars of that distemper which it
was once imagined the royal touch could cure, and by
a slovenly mode of dress. He had the use only of one eye ;
yet so much does mind govern and even supply the defi-
ciency of organs, that his visual perceptions, as far as they
extended, were uncommonly quick and accurate. So
morbid was his temperament, that he never knew the
natural joy of a free and vigorous use of his limbs : when 20

[1] As I do not see any reason to give a different character of my
illustrious friend now, from what I formerly gave, the greatest
part of the sketch of him in my ' Journal of a Tour to the Hebrides '
is here adopted.

B

he walked, it was like the struggling gait of one in fetters ;
when he rode, he had no command or direction of his horse,
but was carried as if in a balloon. That with his constitution and habits of life he should have lived seventy-five
years, is a proof that an inherent *vivida vis* is a powerful
preservative of the human frame.

Man is, in general, made up of contradictory qualities :
and these will ever shew themselves in strange succession,
where a consistency in appearance at least, if not in reality,
10 has not been attained by long habits of philosophical
discipline. In proportion to the native vigour of the mind,
the contradictory qualities will be the more prominent, and
more difficult to be adjusted ; and, therefore, we are not
to wonder, that Johnson exhibited an eminent example of
this remark which I have made upon human nature.   At
different times, he seemed a different man, in some respects :
not, however, in any great or essential article, upon which
he had fully employed his mind, and settled certain principles of duty, but only in his manners, and in the display
20 of argument and fancy in his talk. He was prone to superstition, but not to credulity.   Though his imagination
might incline him to a belief of the marvellous and the
mysterious, his vigorous reason examined the evidence
with jealousy. He was a sincere and zealous Christian, of
high Church-of-England and monarchical principles, which
he would not tamely suffer to be questioned ; and had,
perhaps, at an early period, narrowed his mind somewhat
too much, both as to religion and politicks.   His being
impressed with the danger of extreme latitude in either,
30 though he was of a very independent spirit, occasioned his
appearing somewhat unfavourable to the prevalence of that
noble freedom of sentiment which is the best possession of
man. Nor can it be denied, that he had many prejudices ;
which, however, frequently suggested many of his pointed
sayings, that rather shew a playfulness of fancy than any

settled malignity. He was steady and inflexible in main-
taining the obligations of religion and morality; both from
a regard for the order of society, and from a veneration for
the GREAT SOURCE of all order; correct, nay stern in his
taste; hard to please, and easily offended; impetuous and
irritable in his temper, but of a most humane and benevolent
heart, which shewed itself not only in a most liberal charity,
as far as his circumstances would allow, but in a thousand
instances of active benevolence. He was afflicted with
a bodily disease, which made him often restless and fretful; 10
and with a constitutional melancholy, the clouds of which
darkened the brightness of his fancy, and gave a gloomy
cast to his whole course of thinking: we, therefore, ought
not to wonder at his sallies of impatience and passion at
any time; especially when provoked by obtrusive ignorance, or presuming petulance; and allowance must be
made for his uttering hasty and satirical sallies even against
his best friends. And, surely, when it is considered, that,
' amidst sickness and sorrow ', he exerted his faculties in
so many works for the benefit of mankind, and particularly 20
that he atchieved the great and admirable DICTIONARY of
our language, we must be astonished at his resolution.
The solemn text, ' of him to whom much is given, much
will be required,' seems to have been ever present to his
mind, in a rigorous sense, and to have made him dissatisfied
with his labours and acts of goodness, however comparatively great; so that the unavoidable consciousness
of his superiority was, in that respect, a cause of disquiet.
He suffered so much from this, and from the gloom which
perpetually haunted him, and made solitude frightful, that 30
it may be said of him, ' If in this life only he had hope, he
was of all men most miserable.' He loved praise, when
it was brought to him; but was too proud to seek for
it. He was somewhat susceptible of flattery. As he
was general and unconfined in his studies, he cannot be

considered as master of any one particular science ; but he
had accumulated a vast and various collection of learning
and knowledge, which was so arranged in his mind, as to
be ever in readiness to be brought forth. But his superiority
over other learned men consisted chiefly in what may be
called the art of thinking, the art of using his mind ; a
certain continual power of seizing the useful substance of
all that he knew, and exhibiting it in a clear and forcible
manner ; so that knowledge, which we often see to be no
10 better than lumber in men of dull understanding, was, in
him, true, evident, and actual wisdom. His moral precepts
are practical; for they are drawn from an intimate acquaintance with human nature. His maxims carry conviction ;
for they are founded on the basis of common sense, and
a very attentive and minute survey of real life. His mind
was so full of imagery, that he might have been perpetually
a poet ; yet it is remarkable, that, however rich his prose
is in this respect, his poetical pieces, in general, have not
much of that splendour, but are rather distinguished by
20 strong sentiment, and acute observation, conveyed in harmonious and energetick verse, particularly in heroick
couplets. Though usually grave, and even aweful, in his
deportment, he possessed uncommon and peculiar powers
of wit and humour ; he frequently indulged himself in
colloquial pleasantry ; and the heartiest merriment was
often enjoyed in his company ; with this great advantage,
that as it was entirely free from any poisonous tincture of
vice or impiety, it was salutary to those who shared in it.
He had accustomed himself to such accuracy in his common
30 conversation,[1] that he at all times expressed his thoughts

[1] Though a perfect resemblance of Johnson is not to be found in
any age, parts of his character are admirably expressed by Clarendon, in drawing that of Lord Falkland, whom the noble and
masterly historian describes at his seat near Oxford :—' Such an
immenseness of wit, such a solidity of judgement, so infinite

with great force, and an elegant choice of language, the effect of which was aided by his having a loud voice, and a slow deliberate utterance. In him were united a most logical head with a most fertile imagination, which gave him an extraordinary advantage in arguing : for he could reason close or wide, as he saw best for the moment. Exulting in his intellectual strength and dexterity, he could, when he pleased, be the greatest sophist that ever contended in the lists of declamation ; and, from a spirit of contradiction, and a delight in shewing his powers, he would often main-10 tain the wrong side with equal warmth and ingenuity ; so that, when there was an audience, his real opinions could seldom be gathered from his talk ; though when he was in company with a single friend, he would discuss a subject with genuine fairness : but he was too con-scientious to make errour permanent and pernicious, by deliberately writing it ; and in all his numerous works, he earnestly inculcated what appeared to him to be the truth ; his piety being constant, and the ruling principle of all his conduct.   20

Such was SAMUEL JOHNSON, a man whose talents, acquirements, and virtues, were so extraordinary, that the more his character is considered, the more he will be regarded by the present age, and by posterity, with admira-tion and reverence.

a fancy, bound in by a most logical ratiocination.—His acquain-tance was cultivated by the most polite and accurate men, so that his house was an University in less volume, whither they came, not so much for repose as study, and to examine and refine those grosser propositions, which laziness and consent made current in conversation.'

II

THOMAS BABINGTON, LORD MACAULAY'S *LIFE OF JOHNSON*

First published in the Encyclopaedia Britannica *in 1856.*

SAMUEL JOHNSON, one of the most eminent English writers of the eighteenth century, was the son of Michael Johnson, who was, at the beginning of that century, a magistrate of Lichfield, and a bookseller of great note in the midland counties. Michael's abilities and attainments seem to have been considerable. He was so well acquainted with the contents of the volumes which he exposed to sale, that the country rectors of Staffordshire and Worcestershire thought him an oracle on points of learning. Between
10 him and the clergy, indeed, there was a strong religious and political sympathy. He was a zealous churchman, and, though he had qualified himself for municipal office by taking the oaths to the sovereigns in possession, was to the last a Jacobite in heart. At his house, a house which is still pointed out to every traveller who visits Lichfield, Samuel was born on the 18th of September 1709. In the child the physical, intellectual, and moral peculiarities which afterwards distinguished the man were plainly discernible ; great muscular strength accompanied by much
20 awkwardness and many infirmities ; great quickness of parts, with a morbid propensity to sloth and procrastination ; a kind and generous heart, with a gloomy and irritable temper. He had inherited from his ancestors a scrofulous taint, which it was beyond the power of medicine to

remove. His parents were weak enough to believe that the royal touch was a specific for this malady. In his third year he was taken up to London, inspected by the court surgeon, prayed over by the court chaplains, and stroked and presented with a piece of gold by Queen Anne. One of his earliest recollections was that of a stately lady in a diamond stomacher and a long black hood. Her hand was applied in vain. The boy's features, which were originally noble and not irregular, were distorted by his malady. His cheeks were deeply scarred. He lost for a time the sight of one eye ; and he saw but very imperfectly with the other. But the force of his mind overcame every impediment. Indolent as he was, he acquired knowledge with such ease and rapidity, that at every school to which he was sent he was soon the best scholar. From sixteen to eighteen he resided at home, and was left to his own devices. He learned much at this time, though his studies were without guidance and without plan. He ransacked his father's shelves, dipped into a multitude of books, read what was interesting, and passed over what was dull. An ordinary lad would have acquired little or no useful knowledge in such a way ; but much that was dull to ordinary lads was interesting to Samuel. He read little Greek ; for his proficiency in that language was not such that he could take much pleasure in the masters of Attic poetry and eloquence. But he had left school a good Latinist, and he soon acquired, in the large and miscellaneous library of which he now had the command, an extensive knowledge of Latin literature. That Augustan delicacy of taste, which is the boast of the great public schools of England, he never possessed. But he was early familiar with some classical writers, who were quite unknown to the best scholars in the sixth form at Eton. He was peculiarly attracted by the works of the great restorers of learning. Once, while searching for some apples, he found a huge folio volume of Petrarch's works. The name excited his curiosity, and he eagerly devoured hundreds of pages. Indeed, the diction and versification of his own Latin compositions show that he had paid at least as much attention to modern copies from the antique as to the original models.

While he was thus irregularly educating himself, his family was sinking into hopeless poverty. Old Michael Johnson was much better qualified to pore upon books, and to talk about them, than to trade in them. His business declined : his debts increased ; it was with difficulty that the daily expenses of his household were defrayed. It was out of his power to support his son at either university ; but a wealthy neighbour offered assistance ; and, in reliance on promises which proved to be of very little value, Samuel was entered at Pembroke College, Oxford. When the young scholar presented himself to the rulers of that society, they were amazed not more by his ungainly figure and eccentric manners than by the quantity of extensive and curious information which he had picked up during many months of desultory, but not unprofitable study. On the first day of his residence he surprised his teachers by quoting Macrobius ; and one of the most learned among them declared, that he had never known a freshman of equal attainments.

At Oxford, Johnson resided during about three years. He was poor, even to raggedness ; and his appearance excited a mirth and a pity, which were equally intolerable to his haughty spirit. He was driven from the quadrangle of Christ Church by the sneering looks which the members of that aristocratical society cast at the holes in his shoes. Some charitable person placed a new pair at his door ; but he spurned them away in a fury. Distress made him, not servile, but reckless and ungovernable. No opulent gentleman commoner, panting for one-and-twenty, could

have treated the academical authorities with more gross
disrespect. The needy scholar was generally to be seen
under the gate of Pembroke, a gate now adorned with his
effigy, haranguing a circle of lads, over whom, in spite of
his tattered gown and dirty linen, his wit and audacity
gave him an undisputed ascendancy. In every mutiny
against the discipline of the college he was the ringleader.
Much was pardoned, however, to a youth so highly distinguished by abilities and acquirements. He had early
made himself known by turning Pope's Messiah into Latin 10
verse. The style and rhythm, indeed, were not exactly
Virgilian ; but the translation found many admirers, and
was read with pleasure by Pope himself.

The time drew near at which Johnson would, in the
ordinary course of things, have become a Bachelor of Arts :
but he was at the end of his resources. Those promises of
support on which he had relied had not been kept. His
family could do nothing for him. His debts to Oxford
tradesmen were small indeed, yet larger than he could pay.
In the autumn of 1731, he was under the necessity of 20
quitting the university without a degree. In the following
winter his father died. The old man left but a pittance ;
and of that pittance almost the whole was appropriated to
the support of his widow. The property to which Samuel
succeeded amounted to no more than twenty pounds.

His life, during the thirty years which followed, was one
hard struggle with poverty. The misery of that struggle
needed no aggravation, but was aggravated by the sufferings of an unsound body and an unsound mind. Before
the young man left the university, his hereditary malady 30
had broken forth in a singularly cruel form. He had
become an incurable hypochondriac. He said long after
that he had been mad all his life, or at least not perfectly
sane ; and, in truth, eccentricities less strange than his
have often been thought grounds sufficient for absolving

felons, and for setting aside wills. His grimaces, his
gestures, his mutterings, sometimes diverted and sometimes terrified people who did not know him. At a dinner
table he would, in a fit of absence, stoop down and twitch
off a lady's shoe. He would amaze a drawing-room by
suddenly ejaculating a clause of the Lord's Prayer. He
would conceive an unintelligible aversion to a particular
alley, and perform a great circuit rather than see the
hateful place. He would set his heart on touching every
10 post in the streets through which he walked. If by any
chance he missed a post, he would go back a hundred yards
and repair the omission. Under the influence of his disease,
his senses became morbidly torpid, and his imagination
morbidly active. At one time he would stand poring on
the town clock without being able to tell the hour. At
another, he would distinctly hear his mother, who was
many miles off, calling him by his name. But this was not
the worst. A deep melancholy took possession of him, and
gave a dark tinge to all his views of human nature and of
20 human destiny. Such wretchedness as he endured has
driven many men to shoot themselves or drown themselves. But he was under no temptation to commit suicide.
He was sick of life ; but he was afraid of death ; and he
shuddered at every sight or sound which reminded him of
the inevitable hour. In religion he found but little comfort
during his long and frequent fits of dejection ; for his
religion partook of his own character. The light from
heaven shone on him indeed, but not in a direct line, or
with its own pure splendour. The rays had to struggle
30 through a disturbing medium : they reached him refracted,
dulled and discoloured by the thick gloom which had
settled on his soul ; and, though they might be sufficiently
clear to guide him, were too dim to cheer him.

With such infirmities of body and of mind, this celebrated
man was left, at two-and-twenty, to fight his way through

the world. He remained during about five years in the
midland counties. At Lichfield, his birth-place and his
early home, he had inherited some friends and acquired
others. He was kindly noticed by Henry Hervey, a gay
officer of noble family, who happened to be quartered there.
Gilbert Walmesley, registrar of the ecclesiastical court of
the diocese, a man of distinguished parts, learning, and
knowledge of the world, did himself honour by patronizing
the young adventurer, whose repulsive person, unpolished
manners, and squalid garb, moved many of the petty 10
aristocracy of the neighbourhood to laughter or to disgust.
At Lichfield, however, Johnson could find no way of earn-
ing a livelihood. He became usher of a grammar school
in Leicestershire ; he resided as a humble companion in
the house of a country gentleman ; but a life of dependence
was insupportable to his haughty spirit. He repaired to
Birmingham, and there earned a few guineas by literary
drudgery. In that town he printed a translation, little
noticed at the time, and long forgotten, of a Latin book
about Abyssinia. He then put forth proposals for publish- 20
ing by subscription the poems of Politian, with notes
containing a history of modern Latin verse ; but subscriptions did not come in ; and the volume never appeared.

While leading this vagrant and miserable life, Johnson
fell in love. The object of his passion was Mrs. Elizabeth
Porter, a widow who had children as old as himself. To
ordinary spectators, the lady appeared to be a short, fat,
coarse woman, painted half an inch thick, dressed in gaudy
colours, and fond of exhibiting provincial airs and graces
which were not exactly those of the Queensberrys and 30
Lepels. To Johnson, however, whose passions were strong,
whose eyesight was too weak to distinguish ceruse from
natural bloom, and who had seldom or never been in the
same room with a woman of real fashion, his Titty, as he
called her, was the most beautiful, graceful, and accom-

plished of her sex. That his admiration was unfeigned cannot be doubted ; for she was as poor as himself. She accepted, with a readiness which did her little honour, the addresses of a suitor who might have been her son. The marriage, however, in spite of occasional wranglings, proved happier than might have been expected. The lover continued to be under the illusions of the wedding-day, till the lady died in her sixty-fourth year. On her monument he placed an inscription extolling the charms of her person 10 and of her manners ; and when, long after her decease, he had occasion to mention her, he exclaimed, with a tenderness half ludicrous, half pathetic, ' Pretty creature ! '

His marriage made it necessary for him to exert himself more strenuously than he had hitherto done. He took a house in the neighbourhood of his native town, and advertised for pupils. But eighteen months passed away ; and only three pupils came to his academy. Indeed, his appearance was so strange, and his temper so violent, that his schoolroom must have resembled an ogre's den. Nor 20 was the tawdry painted grandmother whom he called his Titty, well qualified to make provision for the comfort of young gentlemen. David Garrick, who was one of the pupils, used many years later, to throw the best company of London into convulsions of laughter by mimicking the endearments of this extraordinary pair.

At length Johnson, in the twenty-eighth year of his age, determined to seek his fortune in the capital as a literary adventurer. He set out with a few guineas, three acts of the tragedy of Irene in manuscript, and two or three letters 30 of introduction from his friend Walmesley.

Never since literature became a calling in England had it been a less gainful calling than at the time when Johnson took up his residence in London. In the preceding generation a writer of eminent merit was sure to be munificently rewarded by the government. The least that he could

expect was a pension or a sinecure place ; and, if he showed
any aptitude for politics, he might hope to be a member of
parliament, a lord of the treasury, an ambassador, a secretary of state. It would be easy, on the other hand, to name
several writers of the nineteenth century of whom the least
successful has received forty thousand pounds from the
booksellers. But Johnson entered on his vocation in the
most dreary part of the dreary interval which separated
two ages of prosperity. Literature had ceased to flourish
under the patronage of the great, and had not begun to 10
flourish under the patronage of the public. One man of
letters, indeed, Pope, had acquired by his pen what was
then considered as a handsome fortune, and lived on
a footing of equality with nobles and ministers of state.
But this was a solitary exception. Even an author whose
reputation was established, and whose works were popular,
such an author as Thomson, whose Seasons were in every
library, such an author as Fielding, whose Pasquin had
had a greater run than any drama since the Beggar's
Opera, was sometimes glad to obtain, by pawning his best 20
coat, the means of dining on tripe at a cookshop under-
ground, where he could wipe his hands, after his greasy
meal, on the back of a Newfoundland dog. It is easy,
therefore, to imagine what humiliations and privations
must have awaited the novice who had still to earn a name.
One of the publishers to whom Johnson applied for employment measured with a scornful eye that athletic though
uncouth frame, and exclaimed, ' You had better get a
porter's knot, and carry trunks.' Nor was the advice
bad, for a porter was likely to be as plentifully fed, and as 30
comfortably lodged, as a poet.

Some time appears to have elapsed before Johnson was
able to form any literary connection from which he could
expect more than bread for the day which was passing over
him. He never forgot the generosity with which Hervey,

who was now residing in London, relieved his wants during this time of trial. 'Harry Hervey', said the old philosopher many years later, 'was a vicious man ; but he was very kind to me. If you call a dog Hervey, I shall love him.' At Hervey's table Johnson sometimes enjoyed feasts which were made more agreeable by contrast. But in general he dined, and thought that he dined well, on sixpennyworth of meat, and a pennyworth of bread at an alehouse near Drury Lane.

10   The effect of the privations and sufferings which he endured at this time was discernible to the last in his temper and his deportment. His manners had never been courtly. They now became almost savage. Being frequently under the necessity of wearing shabby coats and dirty shirts, he became a confirmed sloven. Being often very hungry when he sate down to his meals, he contracted a habit of eating with ravenous greediness. Even to the end of his life, and even at the tables of the great, the sight of food affected him as it affects wild beasts and 20 birds of prey. His taste in cookery, formed in subterranean ordinaries and *Alamode* beef-shops, was far from delicate. Whenever he was so fortunate as to have near him a hare that had been kept too long, or a meat pie made with rancid butter, he gorged himself with such violence that his veins swelled, and the moisture broke out on his forehead. The affronts which his poverty emboldened stupid and low-minded men to offer to him, would have broken a mean spirit into sycophancy, but made him rude even to ferocity. Unhappily the insolence which, while it was 30 defensive, was pardonable, and in some sense respectable, accompanied him into societies where he was treated with courtesy and kindness. He was repeatedly provoked into striking those who had taken liberties with him. All the sufferers, however, were wise enough to abstain from talking about their beatings, except Osborne, the most rapacious

and brutal of booksellers, who proclaimed everywhere that he had been knocked down by the huge fellow whom he had hired to puff the Harleian Library.

About a year after Johnson had begun to reside in London, he was fortunate enough to obtain regular employment from Cave, an enterprising and intelligent bookseller, who was proprietor and editor of the Gentleman's Magazine. That journal, just entering on the ninth year of its long existence, was the only periodical work in the kingdom which then had what would now be called a large circula- 10 tion. It was indeed, the chief source of parliamentary intelligence. It was not then safe, even during a recess, to publish an account of the proceedings of either House without some disguise. Cave, however, ventured to entertain his readers with what he called Reports of the Debates of the Senate of Lilliput. France was Blefuscu: London was Mildendo: pounds were sprugs: the Duke of Newcastle was the Nardac secretary of state: Lord Hardwicke was the Hugo Hickrad; and William Pulteney was Wingul Pulnub. To write the speeches was, during several years, 20 the business of Johnson. He was generally furnished with notes, meagre indeed, and inaccurate, of what had been said; but sometimes he had to find arguments and eloquence both for the ministry and for the opposition. He was himself a Tory, not from rational conviction—for his serious opinion was that one form of government was just as good or as bad as another—but from mere passion, such as inflamed the Capulets against the Montagues, or the Blues of the Roman circus against the Greens. In his infancy he had heard so much talk about the villanies of the Whigs, 30 and the dangers of the Church, that he had become a furious partisan when he could scarcely speak. Before he was three he had insisted on being taken to hear Sacheverell preach at Lichfield Cathedral, and had listened to the sermon with as much respect, and probably with as much

intelligence, as any Staffordshire squire in the congregation.
The work which had been begun in the nursery had been
completed by the university. Oxford, when Johnson resided there, was the most Jacobitical place in England ;
and Pembroke was one of the most Jacobitical colleges in
Oxford. The prejudices which he brought up to London
were scarcely less absurd than those of his own Tom
Tempest. Charles II. and James II. were two of the best
kings that ever reigned. Laud, a poor creature who never
10 did, said, or wrote any thing indicating more than the
ordinary capacity of an old woman, was a prodigy of parts
and learning over whose tomb Art and Genius still continued to weep. Hampden deserved no more honourable
name than that of 'the zealot of rebellion'. Even the
ship money, condemned not less decidedly by Falkland
and Clarendon than by the bitterest Roundheads, Johnson
would not pronounce to have been an unconstitutional
impost. Under a government the mildest that had ever
been known in the world—under a government which
20 allowed to the people an unprecedented liberty of speech
and action, he fancied that he was a slave ; he assailed the
ministry with obloquy which refuted itself, and regretted
the lost freedom and happiness of those golden days in
which a writer who had taken but one-tenth part of the
license allowed to him would have been pilloried, mangled
with the shears, whipped at the cart's tail, and flung into
a noisome dungeon to die. He hated dissenters and stock-
jobbers, the excise and the army, septennial parliaments,
and continental connections. He long had an aversion to
30 the Scotch, an aversion of which he could not remember
the commencement, but which, he owned, had probably
originated in his abhorrence of the conduct of the nation
during the Great Rebellion. It is easy to guess in what
manner debates on great party questions were likely to be
reported by a man whose judgment was so much disordered

by party spirit. A show of fairness was indeed necessary to the prosperity of the Magazine. But Johnson long afterwards owned that, though he had saved appearances, he had taken care that the Whig dogs should not have the best of it ; and, in fact, every passage which has lived, every passage which bears the marks of his higher faculties, is put into the mouth of some member of the opposition.

A few weeks after Johnson had entered on these obscure labours, he published a work which at once placed him high among the writers of his age. It is probable that 10 what he had suffered during his first year in London had often reminded him of some parts of that noble poem in which Juvenal had described the misery and degradation of a needy man of letters, lodged among the pigeons' nests in the tottering garrets which overhung the streets of Rome. Pope's admirable imitations of Horace's Satires and Epistles had recently appeared, were in every hand, and were by many readers thought superior to the originals. What Pope had done for Horace, Johnson aspired to do for Juvenal. The enterprise was bold, and yet judicious. 20 For between Johnson and Juvenal there was much in common, much more certainly than between Pope and Horace.

Johnson's London appeared without his name in May 1738. He received only ten guineas for this stately and vigorous poem : but the sale was rapid, and the success complete. A second edition was required within a week. Those small critics who are always desirous to lower established reputations ran about proclaiming that the anonymous satirist was superior to Pope in Pope's own 30 peculiar department of literature. It ought to be remembered, to the honour of Pope, that he joined heartily in the applause with which the appearance of a rival genius was welcomed. He made inquiries about the author of London. Such a man, he said, could not long be concealed.

The name was soon discovered; and Pope, with great kindness, exerted himself to obtain an academical degree and the mastership of a grammar school for the poor young poet. The attempt failed, and Johnson remained a bookseller's hack.

It does not appear that these two men, the most eminent writer of the generation which was going out, and the most eminent writer of the generation which was coming in, ever saw each other. They lived in very different circles, one surrounded by dukes and earls, the other by starving pamphleteers and index-makers. Among Johnson's associates at this time may be mentioned Boyse, who, when his shirts were pledged, scrawled Latin verses sitting up in bed with his arms through two holes in his blankets; who composed very respectable sacred poetry when he was sober, and who was at last run over by a hackney coach when he was drunk; Hoole, surnamed the metaphysical tailor, who, instead of attending to his measures, used to trace geometrical diagrams on the board where he sate cross-legged; and the penitent imposter, George Psalmanazar, who, after poring all day, in a humble lodging, on the folios of Jewish rabbis and Christian fathers, indulged himself at night with literary and theological conversation at an alehouse in the city. But the most remarkable of the persons with whom at this time Johnson consorted, was Richard Savage, an earl's son, a shoemaker's apprentice, who had seen life in all its forms, who had feasted among blue ribbands in Saint James's Square, and had lain with fifty pounds weight of irons on his legs, in the condemned ward of Newgate. This man had, after many vicissitudes of fortune, sunk at last into abject and hopeless poverty. His pen had failed him. His patrons had been taken away by death, or estranged by the riotous profusion with which he squandered their bounty, and the ungrateful insolence with which he rejected their

advice. He now lived by begging. He dined on venison
and Champagne whenever he had been so fortunate as to
borrow a guinea. If his questing had been unsuccessful,
he appeased the rage of hunger with some scraps of broken
meat, and lay down to rest under the Piazza of Covent
Garden in warm weather, and, in cold weather, as near as
he could get to the furnace of a glass house. Yet, in his
misery, he was still an agreeable companion. He had an
inexhaustible store of anecdotes about that gay and
brilliant world from which he was now an outcast. He 10
had observed the great men of both parties in hours of
careless relaxation, had seen the leaders of opposition
without the mask of patriotism, and had heard the prime
minister roar with laughter and tell stories not over decent.
During some months Savage lived in the closest familiarity
with Johnson ; and then the friends parted, not without
tears. Johnson remained in London to drudge for Cave.
Savage went to the West of England, lived there as he had
lived everywhere, and, in 1743, died, penniless and heart-
broken, in Bristol gaol.   20

Soon after his death, while the public curiosity was
strongly excited about his extraordinary character, and
his not less extraordinary adventures, a life of him appeared
widely different from the catch-penny lives of eminent
men which were then a staple article of manufacture in
Grub Street. The style was indeed deficient in ease and
variety ; and the writer was evidently too partial to the
Latin element of our language. But the little work, with
all its faults, was a masterpiece. No finer specimen of
literary biography existed in any language, living or dead ; 30
and a discerning critic might have confidently predicted
that the author was destined to be the founder of a new
school of English eloquence.

The Life of Savage was anonymous ; but it was well
known in literary circles that Johnson was the writer.

During the three years which followed, he produced no
important work; but he was not, and indeed could not be,
idle. The fame of his abilities and learning continued to
grow. Warburton pronounced him a man of parts and
genius; and the praise of Warburton was then no light
thing. Such was Johnson's reputation that, in 1747, several
eminent booksellers combined to employ him in the arduous
work of preparing a Dictionary of the English Language,
in two folio volumes. The sum which they agreed to pay
10 him was only fifteen hundred guineas; and out of this sum
he had to pay several poor men of letters who assisted him
in the humbler parts of his task.

The Prospectus of the Dictionary he addressed to the
Earl of Chesterfield. Chesterfield had long been celebrated
for the politeness of his manners, the brilliancy of his wit,
and the delicacy of his taste. He was acknowledged to be
the finest speaker in the House of Lords. He had recently
governed Ireland, at a momentous conjuncture, with
eminent firmness, wisdom, and humanity; and he had
20 since become Secretary of State. He received Johnson's
homage with the most winning affability, and requited it
with a few guineas, bestowed doubtless in a very graceful
manner, but was by no means desirous to see all his carpets
blackened with the London mud, and his soups and wines
thrown to right and left over the gowns of fine ladies and
the waistcoats of fine gentlemen, by an absent, awkward
scholar, who gave strange starts and uttered strange
growls, who dressed like a scarecrow, and ate like a cor-
morant. During some time Johnson continued to call on
30 his patron, but, after being repeatedly told by the porter
that his lordship was not at home, took the hint, and
ceased to present himself at the inhospitable door.

Johnson had flattered himself that he should have completed his Dictionary by the end of 1750; but it was not
till 1755 that he at length gave his huge volumes to the

world. During the seven years which he passed in the
drudgery of penning definitions and marking quotations
for transcription, he sought for relaxation in literary labour
of a more agreeable kind. In 1749 he published the Vanity
of Human Wishes, an excellent imitation of the Tenth
Satire of Juvenal. It is in truth not easy to say whether
the palm belongs to the ancient or to the modern poet.
The couplets in which the fall of Wolsey is described,
though lofty and sonorous, are feeble when compared with
the wonderful lines which bring before us all Rome in 10
tumult on the day of the fall of Sejanus, the laurels on the
door-posts, the white bull stalking towards the Capitol,
the statues rolling down from their pedestals, the flatterers
of the disgraced minister running to see him dragged with
a hook through the streets, and to have a kick at his carcass
before it is hurled into the Tiber. It must be owned too
that in the concluding passage the Christian moralist has
not made the most of his advantages, and has fallen
decidedly short of the sublimity of his Pagan model. On
the other hand, Juvenal's Hannibal must yield to Johnson's 20
Charles; and Johnson's vigorous and pathetic enumera-
tion of the miseries of a literary life must be allowed to be
superior to Juvenal's lamentation over the fate of Demosthenes and Cicero.

For the copyright of the Vanity of Human Wishes
Johnson received only fifteen guineas.

A few days after the publication of this poem, his tragedy,
begun many years before, was brought on the stage. His
pupil, David Garrick, had, in 1741, made his appearance
on a humble stage in Goodman's fields, had at once risen 30
to the first place among actors, and was now, after several
years of almost uninterrupted success, manager of Drury
Lane Theatre. The relation between him and his old
preceptor was of a very singular kind. They repelled each
other strongly, and yet attracted each other strongly.

Nature had made them of very different clay; and circumstances had fully brought out the natural peculiarities of
both.   Sudden prosperity had turned Garrick's head.
Continued adversity had soured Johnson's temper.   Johnson saw with more envy than became so great a man the
villa, the plate, the china, the Brussels carpet, which the
little mimic had got by repeating, with grimaces and
gesticulations, what wiser men had written; and the
exquisitely sensitive vanity of Garrick was galled by
10 the thought that, while all the rest of the world was applaud-
ing him, he could obtain from one morose cynic, whose
opinion it was impossible to despise, scarcely any compliment not acidulated with scorn.   Yet the two Lichfield
men had so many early recollections in common, and
sympathized with each other on so many points on which
they sympathized with nobody else in the vast population
of the capital, that, though the master was often provoked
by the monkey-like impertinence of the pupil, and the
pupil by the bearish rudeness of the master, they remained
20 friends till they were parted by death.   Garrick now brought
Irene out, with alterations sufficient to displease the author,
yet not sufficient to make the piece pleasing to the audience.
The public, however, listened, with little emotion, but with
much civility, to five acts of monotonous declamation.
After nine representations the play was withdrawn.   It is,
indeed, altogether unsuited to the stage, and, even when
perused in the closet, will be found hardly worthy of the
author.   He had not the slightest notion of what blank
verse should be.   A change in the last syllable of every
30 other line would make the versification of the Vanity of
Human Wishes closely resemble the versification of Irene.
The poet, however, cleared, by his benefit nights, and by
the sale of the copyright of his tragedy, about three hundred
pounds, then a great sum in his estimation.

About a year after the representation of Irene, he began

to publish a series of short essays on morals, manners, and literature. This species of composition had been brought into fashion by the success of the Tatler, and by the still more brilliant success of the Spectator. A crowd of small writers had vainly attempted to rival Addison. The Lay Monastery, the Censor, the Freethinker, the Plain Dealer, the Champion, and other works of the same kind, had had their short day. None of them had obtained a permanent place in our literature ; and they are now to be found only in the libraries of the curious. At length 10 Johnson undertook the adventure in which so many aspirants had failed. In the thirty-sixth year after the appearance of the last number of the Spectator, appeared the first number of the Rambler. From March 1750 to March 1752 this paper continued to come out every Tuesday and Saturday.

From the first the Rambler was enthusiastically admired by a few eminent men. Richardson, when only five numbers had appeared, pronounced it equal, if not superior to the Spectator. Young and Hartley expressed their 20 approbation not less warmly. Bubb Dodington, among whose many faults indifference to the claims of genius and learning cannot be reckoned, solicited the acquaintance of the writer. In consequence probably of the good offices of Dodington, who was then the confidential adviser of Prince Frederick, two of his Royal Highness's gentlemen carried a gracious message to the printing-office, and ordered seven copies for Leicester House. But these overtures seem to have been very coldly received. Johnson had had enough of the patronage of the great to last him all his life, and was 30 not disposed to haunt any other door as he had haunted the door of Chesterfield.

By the public the Rambler was at first very coldly received. Though the price of a number was only two-pence, the sale did not amount to five hundred. The profits

were therefore very small. But as soon as the flying leaves
were collected and reprinted they became popular. The
author lived to see thirteen thousand copies spread over
England alone. Separate editions were published for the
Scotch and Irish markets. A large party pronounced the
style perfect, so absolutely perfect that in some essays it
would be impossible for the writer himself to alter a single
word for the better. Another party, not less numerous,
vehemently accused him of having corrupted the purity of
10 the English tongue. The best critics admitted that his
diction was too monotonous, too obviously artificial, and
now and then turgid even to absurdity. But they did
justice to the acuteness of his observations on morals and
manners, to the constant precision and frequent brilliancy
of his language, to the weighty and magnificent eloquence
of many serious passages, and to the solemn yet pleasing
humour of some of the lighter papers. On the question
of precedence between Addison and Johnson, a question
which, seventy years ago, was much disputed, posterity
20 has pronounced a decision from whi h there is no appeal.
Sir Roger, his chaplain and his butier, Will Wimble and
Will Honeycomb, the Vision of Mirza, the Journal of the
Retired Citizen, the Everlasting Club, the Dunmow Flitch,
the Loves of Hilpah and Shalum, the Visit to the Exchange,
and the Visit to the Abbey, are known to everybody. But
many men and women, even of highly cultivated minds,
are unacquainted with Squire Bluster and Mrs. Busy,
Quisquilius and Venustulus, the Allegory of Wit and Learning, the Chronicle of the Revolutions of a Garret, and the
30 sad fate of Aningait and Ajut.

The last Rambler was written in a sad and gloomy hour.
Mrs. Johnson had been given over by the physicians. Three
days later she died. She left her husband almost broken-
hearted. Many people had been surprised to see a man of
his genius and learning stooping to every drudgery, and

denying himself almost every comfort, for the purpose of supplying a silly, affected old woman with superfluities, which she accepted with but little gratitude. But all his affection had been concentrated on her. He had neither brother nor sister, neither son nor daughter. To him she was beautiful as the Gunnings, and witty as Lady Mary. Her opinion of his writings was more important to him than the voice of the pit of Drury Lane Theatre, or the judgment of the Monthly Review. The chief support which had sustained him through the most arduous labour 10 of his life was the hope that she would enjoy the fame and the profit which he anticipated from his Dictionary. She was gone ; and in that vast labyrinth of streets, peopled by eight hundred thousand human beings, he was alone. Yet it was necessary for him to set himself, as he expressed it, doggedly to work. After three more laborious years, the Dictionary was at length complete.

It had been generally supposed that this great work would be dedicated to the eloquent and accomplished nobleman to whom the Prospectus had been addressed. 20 He well knew the value of such a compliment ; and therefore, when the day of publication drew near, he exerted himself to soothe, by a show of zealous and at the same time of delicate and judicious kindness, the pride which he had so cruelly wounded. Since the Ramblers had ceased to appear, the town had been entertained by a journal called The World, to which many men of high rank and fashion contributed. In two successive numbers of the World, the Dictionary was, to use the modern phrase, puffed with wonderful skill. The writings of Johnson were 30 warmly praised. It was proposed that he should be invested with the authority of a Dictator, nay, of a Pope, over our language, and that his decisions about the meaning and the spelling of words should be received as final. His two folios, it was said, would of course be bought by

everybody who could afford to buy them. It was soon
known that these papers were written by Chesterfield.
But the just resentment of Johnson was not to be so
appeased.   In a letter written with singular energy and
dignity of thought and language, he repelled the tardy
advances of his patron. The Dictionary came forth without
a dedication. In the preface the author truly declared that
he owed nothing to the great, and described the difficulties
with which he had been left to struggle so forcibly and
10 pathetically that the ablest and most malevolent of all
the enemies of his fame, Horne Tooke, never could read
that passage without tears.

The public, on this occasion, did Johnson full justice,
and something more than justice. The best lexicographer
may well be content if his productions are received by the
world with cold esteem. But Johnson's Dictionary was
hailed with an enthusiasm such as no similar work has ever
excited. It was indeed the first dictionary which could be
read with pleasure. The definitions show so much acute-
20 ness of thought and command of language, and the passages
quoted from poets, divines, and philosophers, are so skil-
fully selected, that a leisure hour may always be very
agreeably spent in turning over the pages. The faults of
the book resolve themselves, for the most part, into one
great fault. Johnson was a wretched etymologist. He
knew little or nothing of any Teutonic language except
English, which indeed, as he wrote it, was scarcely a
Teutonic language ; and thus he was absolutely at the
mercy of Junius and Skinner.

30   The Dictionary, though it raised Johnson's fame, added
nothing to his pecuniary means. The fifteen hundred
guineas which the booksellers had agreed to pay him had
been advanced and spent before the last sheets issued from
the press. It is painful to relate that, twice in the course
of the year which followed the publication of this great

work, he was arrested and carried to spunging-houses, and that he was twice indebted for his liberty to his excellent friend Richardson. It was still necessary for the man who had been formally saluted by the highest authority as Dictator of the English language to supply his wants by constant toil. He abridged his Dictionary. He proposed to bring out an edition of Shakspeare by subscription ; and many subscribers sent in their names, and laid down their money ; but he soon found the task so little to his taste that he turned to more attractive employments. He 10 contributed many papers to a new monthly journal, which was called the Literary Magazine. Few of these papers have much interest ; but among them was the very best thing that he ever wrote, a masterpiece both of reasoning and of satirical pleasantry, the review of Jenyns's Inquiry into the Nature and Origin of Evil.

In the spring of 1758 Johnson put forth the first of a series of essays, entitled the Idler. During two years these essays continued to appear weekly. They were eagerly read, widely circulated, and, indeed, impudently 20 pirated while they were still in the original form, and had a large sale when collected into volumes. The Idler may be described as a second part of the Rambler, somewhat livelier and somewhat weaker than the first part.

While Johnson was busied with his Idlers, his mother, who had accomplished her ninetieth year, died at Lichfield. It was long since he had seen her ; but he had not failed to contribute largely, out of his small means, to her comfort. In order to defray the charges of her funeral, and to pay some debts which she had left, he wrote a little book in 30 a single week, and sent off the sheets to the press without reading them over. A hundred pounds were paid him for the copyright ; and the purchasers had great cause to be pleased with their bargain ; for the book was Rasselas.

The success of Rasselas was great, though such ladies as

Miss Lydia Languish must have been grievously disappointed when they found that the new volume from the
circulating library was little more than a dissertation on
the author's favourite theme, the Vanity of Human Wishes ;
that the Prince of Abyssinia was without a mistress, and
the Princess without a lover ; and that the story set the
hero and the heroine down exactly where it had taken
them up. The style was the subject of much eager controversy. The Monthly Review and the Critical Review
10 took different sides. Many readers pronounced the writer
a pompous pedant, who would never use a word of two
syllables where it was possible to use a word of six, and
who could not make a waiting woman relate her adventures
without balancing every noun with another noun, and
every epithet with another epithet. Another party, not
less zealous, cited with delight numerous passages in which
weighty meaning was expressed with accuracy and illustrated with splendour. And both the censure and the
praise were merited.

20   About the plan of Rasselas little was said by the critics ;
and yet the faults of the plan might seem to invite severe
criticism. Johnson has frequently blamed Shakspeare for
neglecting the proprieties of time and place, and for ascrib-
ing to one age or nation the manners and opinions of
another. Yet Shakspeare has not sinned in this way more
grievously than Johnson. Rasselas and Imlac, Nekayah
and Pekuah, are evidently meant to be Abyssinians of the
eighteenth century : for the Europe which Imlac describes
is the Europe of the eighteenth century : and the inmates
30 of the Happy Valley talk familiarly of that law of gravita-
tion which Newton discovered, and which was not fully
received even at Cambridge till the eighteenth century.
What a real company of Abyssinians would have been
may be learned from Bruce's Travels. But Johnson, not
content with turning filthy savages ignorant of their

letters, and gorged with raw steaks cut from living cows, into philosophers as eloquent and enlightened as himself or his friend Burke, and into ladies as highly accomplished as Mrs. Lennox or Mrs. Sheridan, transferred the whole domestic system of England to Egypt. Into a land of harems, a land of polygamy, a land where women are married without ever being seen, he introduced the flirtations and jealousies of our ball-rooms. In a land where there is boundless liberty of divorce, wedlock is described as the indissoluble compact. ' A youth and maiden meet- 10 ing by chance, or brought together by artifice, exchange glances, reciprocate civilities, go home and dream of each other. Such ', says Rasselas, ' is the common process of marriage.' Such it may have been, and may still be, in London, but assuredly not at Cairo. A writer who was guilty of such improprieties had little right to blame the poet who made Hector quote Aristotle, and represented Julio Romano as flourishing in the days of the oracle of Delphi.

By such exertions as have been described, Johnson sup- 20 ported himself till the year 1762. In that year a great change in his circumstances took place. He had from a child been an enemy of the reigning dynasty. His Jacobite prejudices had been exhibited with little disguise both in his works and in his conversation. Even in his massy and elaborate Dictionary, he had, with a strange want of taste and judgment, inserted bitter and contumelious reflections on the Whig party. The excise, which was a favourite resource of Whig financiers, he had designated as a hateful tax. He had railed against the commissioners of excise in 30 language so coarse that they had seriously thought of prosecuting him. He had with difficulty been prevented from holding up the Lord Privy Seal by name as an example of the meaning of the word 'renegade'. A pension he had defined as pay given to a state hireling to betray his country ; a pensioner as a slave of state hired by a stipend to obey a master. It seemed unlikely that the author of these definitions would himself be pensioned. But that was a time of wonders. George the Third had ascended the throne ; and had, in the course of a few months, disgusted many of the old friends, and conciliated many of the old enemies of his house. The city was becoming mutinous. Oxford was becoming loyal. Cavendishes and Bentincks were murmuring. Somersets and Wyndhams were hastening to kiss hands. The head of the treasury was now Lord Bute, who was a Tory, and could have no objection to Johnson's Toryism. Bute wished to be thought a patron of men of letters ; and Johnson was one of the most eminent and one of the most needy men of letters in Europe. A pension of three hundred a year was graciously offered, and with very little hesitation accepted.

This event produced a change in Johnson's whole way of life. For the first time since his boyhood he no longer felt the daily goad urging him to the daily toil. He was at liberty, after thirty years of anxiety and drudgery, to indulge his constitutional indolence, to lie in bed till two in the afternoon, and to sit up talking till four in the morning, without fearing either the printer's devil or the sheriff's officer.

One laborious task indeed he had bound himself to perform. He had received large subscriptions for his promised edition of Shakspeare ; he had lived on those subscriptions during some years ; and he could not without disgrace omit to perform his part of the contract. His friends repeatedly exhorted him to make an effort ; and he repeatedly resolved to do so. But, notwithstanding their exhortations and his resolutions, month followed month, year followed year, and nothing was done. He prayed fervently against his idleness ; he determined, as often as he received the sacrament, that he would no longer

doze away and trifle away his time ; but the spell under
which he lay resisted prayer and sacrament. His private
notes at this time are made up of self-reproaches. ' My
indolence', he wrote on Easter eve in 1764, 'has sunk into
grosser sluggishness. A kind of strange oblivion has over-
spread me, so that I know not what has become of the
last year.' Easter 1765 came, and found him still in the
same state. 'My time', he wrote, ' has been unprofitably
spent, and seems as a dream that has left nothing behind.
My memory grows confused, and I know not how the days 10
pass over me.' Happily for his honour, the charm which
held him captive was at length broken by no gentle or
friendly hand. He had been weak enough to pay serious
attention to a story about a ghost which haunted a house
in Cock Lane, and had actually gone himself, with some of
his friends, at one in the morning, to St. John's Church,
Clerkenwell, in the hope of receiving a communication from
the perturbed spirit. But the spirit, though adjured with
all solemnity, remained obstinately silent ; and it soon
appeared that a naughty girl of eleven had been amusing 20
herself by making fools of so many philosophers. Churchill,
who, confident in his powers, drunk with popularity, and
burning with party spirit, was looking for some man of
established fame and Tory politics to insult, celebrated the
Cock Lane Ghost in three cantos, nicknamed Johnson
Pomposo, asked where the book was which had been so
long promised and so liberally paid for, and directly accused
the great moralist of cheating. This terrible word proved
effectual ; and in October 1765 appeared, after a delay of
nine years, the new edition of Shakspeare.   30

This publication saved Johnson's character for honesty,
but added nothing to the fame of his abilities and learning.
The preface, though it contains some good passages, is not
in his best manner. The most valuable notes are those in
which he had an opportunity of showing how attentively

he had during many years observed human life and human nature. The best specimen is the note on the character of Polonius. Nothing so good is to be found even in Wilhelm Meister's admirable examination of Hamlet. But here praise must end. It would be difficult to name a more slovenly, a more worthless edition of any great classic. The reader may turn over play after play without finding one happy conjectural emendation, or one ingenious and satisfactory explanation of a passage which had baffled
10 preceding commentators. Johnson had, in his Prospectus, told the world that he was peculiarly fitted for the task which he had undertaken, because he had, as a lexicographer, been under the necessity of taking a wider view of the English language than any of his predecessors. That his knowledge of our literature was extensive, is indisputable. But, unfortunately, he had altogether neglected that very part of our literature with which it is especially desirable that an editor of Shakspeare should be conversant. It is dangerous to assert a negative. Yet little will be risked
20 by the assertion, that in the two folio volumes of the English Dictionary there is not a single passage quoted from any dramatist of the Elizabethan age, except Shakspeare and Ben. Even from Ben the quotations are few. Johnson might easily, in a few months, have made himself well acquainted with every old play that was extant. But it never seems to have occurred to him that this was a necessary preparation for the work which he had undertaken. He would doubtless have admitted that it would be the height of absurdity in a man who was not familiar
30 with the works of Æschylus and Euripides to publish an edition of Sophocles. Yet he ventured to publish an edition of Shakspeare, without having ever in his life, as far as can be discovered, read a single scene of Massinger, Ford, Decker, Webster, Marlow, Beaumont, or Fletcher. His detractors were noisy and scurrilous. Those who most

loved and honoured him had little to say in praise of the
manner in which he had discharged the duty of a com-
mentator. He had, however, acquitted himself of a debt
which had long lain heavy on his conscience, and he sank
back into the repose from which the sting of satire had
roused him. He long continued to live upon the fame
which he had already won. He was honoured by the
University of Oxford with a Doctor's degree, by the Royal
Academy with a professorship, and by the King with an
interview, in which his Majesty most graciously expressed 10
a hope that so excellent a writer would not cease to write.
In the interval, however, between 1765 and 1775, Johnson
published only two or three political tracts, the longest of
which he could have produced in forty-eight hours, if he
had worked as he worked on the life of Savage and on
Rasselas.

But though his pen was now idle his tongue was active.
The influence exercised by his conversation, directly upon
those with whom he lived, and indirectly on the whole
literary world, was altogether without a parallel. His 20
colloquial talents were indeed of the highest order. He
had strong sense, quick discernment, wit, humour, immense
knowledge of literature and of life, and an infinite store of
curious anecdotes. As respected style, he spoke far better
than he wrote. Every sentence which dropped from his
lips was as correct in structure as the most nicely balanced
period of the Rambler. But in his talk there were no
pompous triads, and little more than a fair proportion of
words in *osity* and *ation*. All was simplicity, ease, and
vigour. He uttered his short, weighty, and pointed 30
sentences with a power of voice, and a justness and energy
of emphasis, of which the effect was rather increased than
diminished by the rollings of his huge form, and by the
asthmatic gaspings and puffings in which the peals of his
eloquence generally ended. Nor did the laziness which

made him unwilling to sit down to his desk prevent him from giving instruction or entertainment orally. To discuss questions of taste, of learning, of casuistry, in language so exact and so forcible that it might have been printed without the alteration of a word, was to him no exertion, but a pleasure. He loved, as he said, to fold his legs and have his talk out. He was ready to bestow the over-flowings of his full mind on anybody who would start a subject, on a fellow-passenger in a stage coach, or on the
10 person who sate at the same table with him in an eating-house. But his conversation was nowhere so brilliant and striking as when he was surrounded by a few friends, whose abilities and knowledge enabled them, as he once expressed it, to send him back every ball that he threw. Some of these, in 1764, formed themselves into a club, which gradually became a formidable power in the common-wealth of letters. The verdicts pronounced by this con-clave on new books were speedily known over all London, and were sufficient to sell off a whole edition in a day, or
20 to condemn the sheets to the service of the trunk-maker and the pastrycook. Nor shall we think this strange when we consider what great and various talents and acquire-ments met in the little fraternity. Goldsmith was the representative of poetry and light literature, Reynolds of the arts, Burke of political eloquence and political philo-sophy. There, too, were Gibbon, the greatest historian, and Jones, the greatest linguist, of the age. Garrick brought to the meetings his inexhaustible pleasantry, his incom-parable mimicry, and his consummate knowledge of stage
30 effect. Among the most constant attendants were two high-born and high-bred gentlemen, closely bound together by friendship, but of widely different characters and habits ; Bennet Langton, distinguished by his skill in Greek litera-ture, by the orthodoxy of his opinions, and by the sanctity of his life ; and Topham Beauclerk, renowned for his

amours, his knowledge of the gay world, his fastidious taste, and his sarcastic wit. To predominate over such a society was not easy. Yet even over such a society Johnson predominated. Burke might indeed have disputed the supremacy to which others were under the necessity of submitting. But Burke, though not generally a very patient listener, was content to take the second part when Johnson was present ; and the club itself, consisting of so many eminent men, is to this day popularly designated as Johnson's Club.   10

Among the members of this celebrated body was one to whom it has owed the greater part of its celebrity, yet who was regarded with little respect by his brethren, and had not without difficulty obtained a seat among them. This was James Boswell, a young Scotch lawyer, heir to an honourable name and a fair estate. That he was a coxcomb and a bore, weak, vain, pushing, curious, garrulous, was obvious to all who were acquainted with him. That he could not reason, that he had no wit, no humour, no eloquence, is apparent from his writings. And yet his writ- 20 ings are read beyond the Mississippi, and under the Southern Cross, and are likely to be read as long as the English exists, either as a living or as a dead language. Nature had made him a slave and an idolater. His mind resembled those creepers which the botanists call parasites, and which can subsist only by clinging round the stems and imbibing the juices of stronger plants. He must have fastened himself on somebody. He might have fastened himself on Wilkes, and have become the fiercest patriot in the Bill of Rights Society. He might have fastened himself on Whitfield, 30 and have become the loudest field preacher among the Calvinistic Methodists. In a happy hour he fastened himself on Johnson. The pair might seem ill matched. For Johnson had early been prejudiced against Boswell's country. To a man of Johnson's strong understanding

and irritable temper, the silly egotism and adulation of
Boswell must have been as teasing as the constant buzz of
a fly. Johnson hated to be questioned ; and Boswell was
eternally catechizing him on all kinds of subjects, and
sometimes propounded such questions as, ' What would
you do, sir, if you were locked up in a tower with a baby ? '
Johnson was a water drinker and Boswell was a winebibber,
and indeed little better than a habitual sot. It was impossible that there should be perfect harmony between two
10 such companions. Indeed, the great man was sometimes
provoked into fits of passion, in which he said things which
the small man, during a few hours, seriously resented.
Every quarrel, however, was soon made up. During
twenty years the disciple continued to worship the master :
the master continued to scold the disciple, to sneer at him,
and to love him. The two friends ordinarily resided at
a great distance from each other. Boswell practised in the
Parliament House of Edinburgh, and could pay only
occasional visits to London. During those visits his chief
20 business was to watch Johnson, to discover all Johnson's
habits, to turn the conversation to subjects about which
Johnson was likely to say something remarkable, and to
fill quarto note-books with minutes of what Johnson had
said. In this way were gathered the materials, out of
which was afterwards constructed the most interesting
biographical work in the world.

Soon after the club began to exist, Johnson formed
a connection less important indeed to his fame, but much
more important to his happiness, than his connection with
30 Boswell. Henry Thrale, one of the most opulent brewers
in the kingdom, a man of sound and cultivated understanding, rigid principles, and liberal spirit, was married to one
of those clever, kind-hearted, engaging, vain, pert, young
women, who are perpetually doing or saying what is not
exactly right, but who, do or say what they may, are

always agreeable. In 1765 the Thrales became acquainted
with Johnson, and the acquaintance ripened fast into
friendship. They were astonished and delighted by the
brilliancy of his conversation. They were flattered by
finding that a man so widely celebrated preferred their
house to any other in London. Even the peculiarities
which seemed to unfit him for civilized society, his gesticulations, his rollings, his puffings, his mutterings, the strange
way in which he put on his clothes, the ravenous eagerness
with which he devoured his dinner, his fits of melancholy, 10
his fits of anger, his frequent rudeness, his occasional
ferocity, increased the interest which his new associates
took in him. For these things were the cruel marks left
behind by a life which had been one long conflict with
disease and with adversity. In a vulgar hack writer, such
oddities would have excited only disgust. But in a man of
genius, learning, and virtue, their effect was to add pity
to admiration and esteem. Johnson soon had an apartment at the brewery in Southwark, and a still more pleasant
apartment at the villa of his friends on Streatham Common. 20
A large part of every year he passed in those abodes—abodes
which must have seemed magnificent and luxurious indeed,
when compared with the dens in which he had generally
been lodged. But his chief pleasures were derived from
what the astronomer of his Abyssinian tale called ' the
endearing elegance of female friendship '. Mrs. Thrale
rallied him, soothed him, coaxed him, and, if she sometimes
provoked him by her flippancy, made ample amends by
listening to his reproofs with angelic sweetness of temper.
When he was diseased in body and in mind, she was the 30
most tender of nurses. No comfort that wealth could
purchase, no contrivance that womanly ingenuity, set to
work by womanly compassion, could devise was wanting
to his sick room. He requited her kindness by an affection
pure as the affection of a father, yet delicately tinged with

a gallantry, which, though awkward, must have been more
flattering than the attentions of a crowd of the fools who
gloried in the names, now obsolete, of Buck and Maccaroni.
It should seem that a full half of Johnson's life, during
about sixteen years, was passed under the roof of the
Thrales. He accompanied the family sometimes to Bath,
and sometimes to Brighton, once to Wales and once to
Paris. But he had at the same time a house in one of the
narrow and gloomy courts on the north of Fleet Street. In
10 the garrets was his library, a large and miscellaneous collection of books, falling to pieces and begrimed with dust.
On a lower floor he sometimes, but very rarely, regaled
a friend with a plain dinner, a veal pie, or a leg of lamb
and spinage, and a rice pudding. Nor was the dwelling
uninhabited during his long absences. It was the home of
the most extraordinary assemblage of inmates that ever
was brought together. At the head of the establishment
Johnson had placed an old lady named Williams, whose
chief recommendations were her blindness and her poverty.
20 But, in spite of her murmurs and reproaches, he gave an
asylum to another lady who was as poor as herself, Mrs.
Desmoulins, whose family he had known many years
before in Staffordshire. Room was found for the daughter
of Mrs. Desmoulins, and for another destitute damsel, who
was generally addressed as Miss Carmichael, but whom her
generous host called Polly. An old quack doctor named
Levett, who bled and dosed coal-heavers and hackney
coachmen, and received for fees crusts of bread, bits of
bacon, glasses of gin, and sometimes a little copper, com-
30 pleted this strange menagerie. All these poor creatures
were at constant war with each other, and with Johnson's
negro servant Frank. Sometimes, indeed, they transferred
their hostilities from the servant to the master, complained
that a better table was not kept for them, and railed or
maundered till their benefactor was glad to make his escape

to Streatham, or to the Mitre Tavern. And yet he, who was generally the haughtiest and most irritable of mankind, who was but too prompt to resent anything which looked like a slight on the part of a purse-proud bookseller, or of a noble and powerful patron, bore patiently from mendicants, who, but for his bounty, must have gone to the workhouse, insults more provoking than those for which he had knocked down Osborne and bidden defiance to Chesterfield. Year after year Mrs. Williams and Mrs. Desmoulins, Polly and Levett, continued to torment him 10 and to live upon him.

The course of life which has been described was interrupted in Johnson's sixty-fourth year by an important event. He had early read an account of the Hebrides, and had been much interested by learning that there was so near him a land peopled by a race which was still as rude and simple as in the middle ages. A wish to become intimately acquainted with a state of society so utterly unlike all that he had ever seen frequently crossed his mind. But it is not probable that his curiosity would 20 have overcome his habitual sluggishness, and his love of the smoke, the mud, and the cries of London, had not Boswell importuned him to attempt the adventure, and offered to be his squire. At length, in August 1773, Johnson crossed the Highland line, and plunged courageously into what was then considered, by most Englishmen, as a dreary and perilous wilderness. After wandering about two months through the Celtic region, sometimes in rude boats which did not protect him from the rain, and sometimes on small shaggy ponies which could hardly bear his weight, 30 he returned to his old haunts with a mind full of new images and new theories. During the following year he employed himself in recording his adventures. About the beginning of 1775, his Journey to the Hebrides was published, and was, during some weeks, the chief subject of conversation

in all circles in which any attention was paid to literature.
The book is still read with pleasure. The narrative is
entertaining ; the speculations, whether sound or unsound,
are always ingenious ; and the style, though too stiff and
pompous, is somewhat easier and more graceful than that
of his early writings. His prejudice against the Scotch
had at length become little more than matter of jest ; and
whatever remained of the old feeling had been effectually
removed by the kind and respectful hospitality with which
10 he had been received in every part of Scotland. It was, of
course, not to be expected that an Oxonian Tory should
praise the Presbyterian polity and ritual, or that an eye
accustomed to the hedgerows and parks of England should
not be struck by the bareness of Berwickshire and East
Lothian. But even in censure Johnson's tone is not
unfriendly. The most enlightened Scotchmen, with Lord
Mansfield at their head, were well pleased. But some
foolish and ignorant Scotchmen were moved to anger by
a little unpalatable truth which was mingled with much
20 eulogy, and assailed him whom they chose to consider as
the enemy of their country with libels much more dis-
honourable to their country than anything that he had
ever said or written. They published paragraphs in the
newspapers, articles in the magazines, sixpenny pamphlets,
five shilling books. One scribbler abused Johnson for being
blear-eyed ; another for being a pensioner ; a third informed the world that one of the Doctor's uncles had been
convicted of felony in Scotland, and had found that there
was in that country one tree capable of supporting the
30 weight of an Englishman. Macpherson, whose Fingal had
been proved in the Journey to be an impudent forgery,
threatened to take vengeance with a cane. The only effect
of this threat was that Johnson reiterated the charge of
forgery in the most contemptuous terms, and walked
about, during some time, with a cudgel, which, if the

impostor had not been too wise to encounter it, would
assuredly have descended upon him, to borrow the sublime
language of his own epic poem, ' like a hammer on the red
son of the furnace.'

Of other assailants Johnson took no notice whatever.
He had early resolved never to be drawn into controversy ;
and he adhered to his resolution with a steadfastness which
is the more extraordinary, because he was, both intellectu-
ally and morally, of the stuff of which controversialists are
made.   In conversation, he was a singularly eager, acute, 10
and pertinacious disputant.   When at a loss for good
reasons, he had recourse to sophistry ; and when heated
by altercation, he made unsparing use of sarcasm and
invective.   But when he took his pen in his hand, his whole
character seemed to be changed.   A hundred bad writers
misrepresented him and reviled him ; but not one of the
hundred could boast of having been thought by him worthy
of a refutation, or even of a retort.   The Kenricks, Camp-
bells, MacNicols, and Hendersons, did their best to annoy
him, in the hope that he would give them importance by 20
answering them.   But the reader will in vain search his
works for any allusion to Kenrick or Campbell, to MacNicol
or Henderson.   One Scotchman, bent on vindicating the
fame of Scotch learning, defied him to the combat in
a detestable Latin hexameter,

> ' Maxime, si tu vis, cupio contendere tecum.'

But Johnson took no notice of the challenge.   He had
learned, both from his own observation and from literary
history, in which he was deeply read, that the place of
books in the public estimation is fixed, not by what is 30
written about them, but by what is written in them ; and
that an author whose works are likely to live is very unwise
if he stoops to wrangle with detractors whose works are
certain to die.   He always maintained that fame was a

shuttlecock which could be kept up only by being beaten back, as well as beaten forward, and which would soon fall if there were only one battledore. No saying was oftener in his mouth than that fine apophthegm of Bentley, that no man was ever written down but by himself.

Unhappily, a few months after the appearance of the Journey to the Hebrides, Johnson did what none of his envious assailants could have done, and to a certain extent succeeded in writing himself down. The disputes between
10 England and her American colonies had reached a point at which no amicable adjustment was possible. Civil war was evidently impending ; and the ministers seem to have thought that the eloquence of Johnson might with advantage be employed to inflame the nation against the opposition here, and against the rebels beyond the Atlantic. He had already written two or three tracts in defence of the foreign and domestic policy of the government; and those tracts, though hardly worthy of him, were much superior to the crowd of pamphlets which lay on the counters of Almon
20 and Stockdale. But his Taxation No Tyranny was a pitiable failure. The very title was a silly phrase, which can have been recommended to his choice by nothing but a jingling alliteration which he ought to have despised. The arguments were such as boys use in debating societies. The pleasantry was as awkward as the gambols of a hippopotamus. Even Boswell was forced to own that, in this unfortunate piece, he could detect no trace of his master's powers. The general opinion was that the strong faculties which had produced the Dictionary and the Rambler were
30 beginning to feel the effect of time and of disease, and that the old man would best consult his credit by writing no more.

But this was a great mistake. Johnson had failed, not because his mind was less vigorous than when he wrote Rasselas in the evenings of a week, but because he had foolishly chosen, or suffered others to choose for him,

a subject such as he would at no time have been competent
to treat. He was in no sense a statesman. He never
willingly read or thought or talked about affairs of state.
He loved biography, literary history, the history of manners;
but political history was positively distasteful to him. The
question at issue between the colonies and the mother
country was a question about which he had really nothing
to say. He failed, therefore, as the greatest men must fail
when they attempt to do that for which they are unfit ;
as Burke would have failed if Burke had tried to write 10
comedies like those of Sheridan ; as Reynolds would have
failed if Reynolds had tried to paint landscapes like those
of Wilson. Happily, Johnson soon had an opportunity of
proving most signally that his failure was not to be ascribed
to intellectual decay.

On Easter eve 1777, some persons, deputed by a meeting
which consisted of forty of the first booksellers in London,
called upon him. Though he had some scruples about
doing business at that season, he received his visitors with
much civility. They came to inform him that a new 20
edition of the English poets, from Cowley downwards, was
in contemplation, and to ask him to furnish short biographical prefaces. He readily undertook the task, a task
for which he was pre-eminently qualified. His knowledge
of the literary history of England since the Restoration
was unrivalled. That knowledge he had derived partly
from books, and partly from sources which had long been
closed ; from old Grub Street traditions ; from the talk of
forgotten poetasters and pamphleteers who had long been
lying in parish vaults ; from the recollections of such men 30
as Gilbert Walmesley, who had conversed with the wits of
Button ; Cibber, who had mutilated the plays of two
generations of dramatists ; Orrery, who had been admitted
to the society of Swift ; and Savage, who had rendered
services of no very honourable kind to Pope. The bio-

grapher therefore sate down to his task with a mind full of matter. He had at first intended to give only a paragraph to every minor poet, and only four or five pages to the greatest name. But the flood of anecdote and criticism overflowed the narrow channel. The work, which was originally meant to consist only of a few sheets, swelled into ten volumes, small volumes, it is true, and not closely printed. The first four appeared in 1779, the remaining six in 1781.

10 The Lives of the Poets are, on the whole, the best of Johnson's works. The narratives are as entertaining as any novel. The remarks on life and on human nature are eminently shrewd and profound. The criticisms are often excellent, and, even when grossly and provokingly unjust, well deserve to be studied. For, however erroneous they may be, they are never silly. They are the judgments of a mind trammelled by prejudice and deficient in sensibility, but vigorous and acute. They, therefore, generally contain a portion of valuable truth which deserves to be separated 20 from the alloy ; and, at the very worst, they mean something, a praise to which much of what is called criticism in our time has no pretensions.

Savage's Life Johnson reprinted nearly as it had appeared in 1744. Whoever, after reading that life, will turn to the other lives will be struck by the difference of style. Since Johnson had been at ease in his circumstances he had written little and had talked much. When, therefore, he, after the lapse of years, resumed his pen, the mannerism which he had contracted while he was in the constant 30 habit of elaborate composition was less perceptible than formerly ; and his diction frequently had a colloquial ease which it had formerly wanted. The improvement may be discerned by a skilful critic in the Journey to the Hebrides, and in the Lives of the Poets is so obvious that it cannot escape the notice of the most careless reader.

Among the Lives the best are perhaps those of Cowley, Dryden, and Pope. The very worst is, beyond all doubt, that of Gray.

This great work at once became popular. There was, indeed, much just and much unjust censure ; but even those who were loudest in blame were attracted by the book in spite of themselves. Malone computed the gains of the publishers at five or six thousand pounds. But the writer was very poorly remunerated. Intending at first to write very short prefaces, he had stipulated for only two 10 hundred guineas. The booksellers, when they saw how far his performance had surpassed his promise, added only another hundred. Indeed, Johnson, though he did not despise, or affect to despise money, and though his strong sense and long experience ought to have qualified him to protect his own interests, seems to have been singularly unskilful and unlucky in his literary bargains. He was generally reputed the first English writer of his time. Yet several writers of his time sold their copyrights for sums such as he never ventured to ask. To give a single instance, 20 Robertson received four thousand five hundred pounds for the history of Charles V. ; and it is no disrespect to the memory of Robertson to say that the History of Charles V. is both a less valuable and a less amusing book than the Lives of the Poets.

Johnson was now in his seventy-second year. The infirmities of age were coming fast upon him. That inevitable event of which he never thought without horror was brought near to him ; and his whole life was darkened by the shadow of death. He had often to pay the cruel price of 30 longevity. Every year he lost what could never be replaced. The strange dependants to whom he had given shelter, and to whom, in spite of their faults, he was strongly attached by habit, dropped off one by one ; and, in the silence of his home, he regretted even the noise of their

scolding matches. The kind and generous Thrale was no more ; and it would have been well if his wife had been laid beside him. But she survived to be the laughing-stock of those who had envied her, and to draw from the eyes of the old man who had loved her beyond anything in the world, tears far more bitter than he would have shed over her grave. With some estimable, and many agreeable qualities, she was not made to be independent. The control of a mind more stedfast than her own was necessary to her
10 respectability. While she was restrained by her husband, a man of sense and firmness, indulgent to her taste in trifles, but always the undisputed master of his house, her worst offences had been impertinent jokes, white lies, and short fits of pettishness ending in sunny good humour. But he was gone ; and she was left an opulent widow of forty, with strong sensibility, volatile fancy, and slender judgment. She soon fell in love with a music-master from Brescia, in whom nobody but herself could discover any-thing to admire. Her pride, and perhaps some better
20 feelings, struggled hard against this degrading passion. But the struggle irritated her nerves, soured her temper, and at length endangered her health. Conscious that her choice was one which Johnson could not approve, she became desirous to escape from his inspection. Her manner towards him changed. She was sometimes cold and sometimes petulant. She did not conceal her joy when he left Streatham ; she never pressed him to return ; and, if he came unbidden, she received him in a manner which con-vinced him that he was no longer a welcome guest. He took
30 the very intelligible hints which she gave. He read, for the last time, a chapter of the Greek Testament in the library which had been formed by himself. In a solemn and tender prayer he commended the house and its inmates to the Divine protection, and, with emotions which choked his voice and convulsed his powerful frame, left for ever that

beloved home for the gloomy and desolate house behind
Fleet Street, where the few and evil days which still
remained to him were to run out. Here, in June 1783, he
had a paralytic stroke, from which, however, he recovered,
and which does not appear to have at all impaired his
intellectual faculties. But other maladies came thick upon
him. His asthma tormented him day and night. Dropsical
symptoms made their appearance. While sinking under
a complication of diseases, he heard that the woman whose
friendship had been the chief happiness of sixteen years of 10
his life, had married an Italian fiddler ; that all London
was crying shame upon her ; and that the newspapers and
magazines were filled with allusions to the Ephesian matron
and the two pictures in Hamlet. He vehemently said that
he would try to forget her existence. He never uttered
her name. Every memorial of her which met his eye he
flung into the fire. She meanwhile fled from the laughter
and hisses of her countrymen and countrywomen to a land
where she was unknown, hastened across Mount Cenis, and
learned, while passing a merry Christmas of concerts and 20
lemonade parties at Milan, that the great man with whose
name hers is inseparably associated, had ceased to exist.

He had, in spite of much mental and much bodily
affliction, clung vehemently to life. The feeling described
in that fine but gloomy paper which closes the series of his
Idlers seemed to grow stronger in him as his last hour drew
near. He fancied that he should be able to draw his breath
more easily in a southern climate, and would probably
have set out for Rome and Naples but for his fear of the
expense of the journey. That expense, indeed, he had the 30
means of defraying ; for he had laid up about two thousand
pounds, the fruit of labours which had made the fortune
of several publishers. But he was unwilling to break in
upon this hoard, and he seems to have wished even to keep
its existence a secret. Some of his friends hoped that the

government might be induced to increase his pension to six hundred pounds a year, but this hope was disappointed, and he resolved to stand one English winter more. That winter was his last. His legs grew weaker; his breath grew shorter; the fatal water gathered fast, in spite of incisions which he, courageous against pain, but timid against death, urged his surgeons to make deeper and deeper. Though the tender care which had mitigated his sufferings during months of sickness at Streatham was 10 withdrawn, he was not left desolate. The ablest physicians and surgeons attended him, and refused to accept fees from him. Burke parted from him with deep emotion. Windham sate much in the sick room, arranged the pillows, and sent his own servant to watch at night by the bed. Frances Burney, whom the old man had cherished with fatherly kindness, stood weeping at the door; while Langton, whose piety eminently qualified him to be an adviser and com- forter at such a time, received the last pressure of his friend's hand within. When at length the moment, dreaded 20 through so many years, came close, the dark cloud passed away from Johnson's mind. His temper became unusually patient and gentle; he ceased to think with terror of death, and of that which lies beyond death; and he spoke much of the mercy of God, and of the propitiation of Christ. In this serene frame of mind he died on the 13th of December 1784. He was laid, a week later, in Westminster Abbey, among the eminent men of whom he had been the historian,—Cowley and Denham, Dryden and Congreve, Gay, Prior, and Addison.

30   Since his death the popularity of his works—the Lives of the Poets, and, perhaps, the Vanity of Human Wishes, excepted—has greatly diminished. His Dictionary has been altered by editors till it can scarcely be called his. An allusion to his Rambler or his Idler is not readily apprehended in literary circles. The fame even of Rasselas

has grown somewhat dim. But though the celebrity of the writings may have declined, the celebrity of the writer, strange to say, is as great as ever. Boswell's book has done for him more than the best of his own books could do. The memory of other authors is kept alive by their works. But the memory of Johnson keeps many of his works alive. The old philosopher is still among us in the brown coat with the metal buttons and the shirt which ought to be at wash, blinking, puffing, rolling his head, drumming with his fingers, tearing his meat like a tiger, and swallowing 10 his tea in oceans. No human being who has been more than seventy years in the grave is so well known to us. And it is but just to say that our intimate acquaintance with what he would himself have called the anfractuosities of his intellect and of his temper, serves only to strengthen our conviction that he was both a great and a good man.

III

Sir WALTER RALEIGH'S

SAMUEL JOHNSON

The Leslie Stephen Lecture, *delivered in the Senate House,
Cambridge, February 22, 1907 ; printed from* Six
Essays on Johnson *(Oxford, 1910).*

THE honour that the University of Cambridge has done
me by asking me to deliver the first Leslie Stephen lecture
is the best kind of honour, for it appeals even more to
affection than to pride. Like most men whose trade is
lecturing, I have known many Universities ; but none of
them can be so dear to memory as the place of my early
friendships, and dreams, and idleness.

A quarter of a century ago I heard Leslie Stephen
lecture in the Divinity Schools of this place. I saw him
10 once again, on the uplands of Cornwall, but I never again
heard his voice. You will not expect from me, therefore,
any reminiscences, or intimate appreciation of his character.
But I can say something of what I believe was very imperfectly known to him, the regard and reverence that was
felt for him by a younger generation. A busy man of
letters, always occupied with fresh tasks, has little time to
study the opinions of his juniors. He makes his progress
from book to book, without looking back, and knows more of
the pains of doing than of the pleasures of the thing done.
20 Far on in his career, while he is still struggling with his
difficult material, he discovers, to his surprise, that the
younger world regards him as a triumphant dictator and
law-giver. Something of this kind I think happened to

Leslie Stephen. He woke up, late in life, to find himself
an established institution. He was pleased, and half-
incredulous, and he turned to his weary task again. But
indeed he had been famous and influential far longer than
he knew. The work in literary criticism that was done by
him, and by Sir James Fitzjames Stephen, was unlike
most of the criticism of the last age. Amid a crowd of
treatises which directed attention chiefly to the manner
of an author, it was a solid comfort to come across a critic
who made it his business to grasp the matter, and who
paid even a poet the compliment of supposing that he had
something to say. There is no finer literary model than
bare matter of fact ; and Leslie Stephen's style, ' the lean
terse style ' as it has been called, constantly aimed at this
perfection. The *Dictionary of National Biography*, under
his control, became a gymnasium for authors, a gymnasium
where no one was permitted to exercise his muscle until
he had stripped himself of those garments which ordinary
literary society expects authors to wear. It was Leslie
Stephen's aim to prove that this avoidance of superfluity
is not the negation of criticism. He was nothing if not
critical, but he endeavoured to identify his criticism with
the facts, to make it the wall of the building, not a flying
buttress. When he relaxed something of his rigour and
severity, as he did in his latest studies, his ease was like
Dryden's, the ease of an athlete ; and the native qualities
of his mind, his sincerity and kindliness and depth of
feeling, are nowhere more visible than in his latest and best
prose. He still keeps close to his subject, but he permits
himself an indulgence which formerly he refused, and
sometimes, for a few delightful sentences, speaks of
himself.

There is no need for haste in estimating his work and his
services to good letters. These will not soon be forgotten.
I like to think that he would have approved my choice of

a subject for the first of the lectures associated with his name. His enjoyment of books, he said at the close of his life, had begun and ended with Boswell's *Life of Johnson*. Literature, as it is understood for the purposes of these lectures, is to include, so I am informed, biography, criticism, and ethics. If I had been commanded to choose from the world's annals a name which, better than any other, should serve to illustrate the vital relations of those three subjects to literature, I could find no better name than
10 Samuel Johnson. He was himself biographer, critic, and moralist. His life is inseparable from his works ; his morality was the motive power of all that he wrote, and the inspiration of much that he did. Of all great men, dead or alive, he is the best known to us ; yet perhaps he was greater than we know.

The accident which gave Boswell to Johnson and Johnson to Boswell is one of the most extraordinary pieces of good fortune in literary history. Boswell was a man of genius ; the idle paradox which presents him in the likeness of
20 a lucky dunce was never tenable by serious criticism, and has long since been rejected by all who bring thought to bear on the problems of literature. If I had to find a paradox in Boswell I should find it in this, that he was a Scot. His character was destitute of all the vices, and all the virtues, which are popularly, and in the main rightly, attributed to the Scottish people. The young Scot is commonly shy, reserved, and self-conscious ; independent in temper, sensitive to affront, slow to make friends, and wary in society. Boswell was the opposite of all these
30 things. He made himself at home in all societies, and charmed others into a like ease and confidence. Under the spell of his effervescent good-humour the melancholy Highlanders were willing to tell stories of the supernatural. ' Mr. Boswell's frankness and gayety ', says Johnson, ' made everybody communicative.' It was no

small part of Boswell's secret that he talked with engaging freedom, and often, as it seemed, with childish vanity, of himself. He had the art of interesting others without incurring their respect. He had no ulterior motives. He desired no power, only information, so that his companions recognized his harmlessness, and despised him, and talked to him without a shadow of restraint. He felt a sincere and unbounded admiration for greatness or originality of intellect. 'I have the happiness', he wrote to Lord Chatham, ' of being capable to contemplate with supreme 10 delight those distinguished spirits by which God is some-times pleased to honour humanity.' But indeed he did not confine his interest to the great. He was an amateur of human life; his zest in its smallest incidents and his endless curiosity were infectious and irresistible. No scientific investigator has ever been prompted by a livelier zeal for knowledge; and his veracity was scrupulous and absolute. ' A Scotchman must be a very sturdy moralist', said Johnson, ' who does not love Scotland better than truth.' Boswell was very far indeed from being a sturdy 20 moralist, but he loved truth better than Scotland, better even than himself. Most of the stories told against him, and almost all the witticisms reported at his expense, were first narrated by himself. He had simplicity, candour, fervour, a warmly affectionate nature, a quick intelligence, and a passion for telling all that he knew. These are qualities which make for good literature. They enabled Boswell to portray Johnson with an intimacy and truth that has no parallel in any language.

We owe such an enormous debt of gratitude to Boswell 30 that it seems ungrateful to suggest what is nevertheless obviously true, that the Johnson we know best is Boswell's Johnson. The *Life* would be a lesser work than it is if it had not the unity that was imposed upon it by the mind of its writer. The portrait is so broad and masterly, so

nobly conceived and so faithful in detail, that the world
has been content to look at Johnson from this point of
view and no other.   Yet it cannot be denied, and Boswell
himself would have been the first to admit it, that there
are aspects and periods of Johnson's career which are not
and could not be fully treated in the *Life*.   When Johnson
first saw Boswell in Tom Davies's back shop, he was
fifty-four years old and Boswell was twenty-two.   The
year before the meeting Johnson had been rescued, by the
10 grant of an honourable pension, from the prolonged struggle
with poverty which makes up so great a part of the story
of his life.   He had conquered his world ; his circumstances
were now comparatively easy and his primacy was universally acknowledged.   All these facts have left their
mark on Boswell's book.   We have some trivial and slight
memorials of Shakespeare by men who treated him on
equal terms of friendship or rivalry.   But Johnson, in our
conception of him, is always on a pedestal.   He is Doctor
Johnson ; although he was sixty-six years of age when his
20 own University gave him its honorary degree.   The fact
is that we cannot escape from Boswell any more than his
hero could ; and we do not wish to escape, and we do not
try.   There are many admirers and friends of Johnson who
are familiar with every notable utterance recorded by
Boswell, who yet would be hard put to it if they were asked
to quote a single sentence from *The Rambler*.   That splendid
repository of wisdom and truth has ceased to attract
readers : it has failed and has been forgotten in the unequal
contest with Boswell.   ' It is not sufficiently considered,'
30 said Johnson, in an early number of *The Rambler*, ' that men
more frequently require to be reminded than informed.'
I desire to remind you of the work of Johnson, the writer
of prose ; and I am happy in my subject, for the unique
popularity of Boswell has given to the study of Johnson's
own works a certain flavour of novelty and research.

It will be wise to face at once the charge so often brought against these writings, that they are dull. M. Taine, who somehow got hold of the mistaken idea that Johnson's periodical essays are the favourite reading of the English people, has lent his support to this charge. Wishing to know what ideas had made Johnson popular, he turned over the pages of his *Dictionary*, his eight volumes of essays, his biographies, his numberless articles, his conversation so carefully collected, and he yawned. 'His truths', says the critic, 'are too true, we already know his precepts by heart. We learn from him that life is short, and we ought to improve the few moments granted us; that a mother ought not to bring up her son as a fop; that a man ought to repent of his faults and yet avoid superstition; that in everything we ought to be active and not hurried. We thank him for these sage counsels, but we mutter to ourselves that we could have done very well without them.' I will not continue the quotation. It is clear that M. Taine's study of Johnson was limited to a table of contents. What he says amounts to this—that Johnson's writings are a treasury of commonplaces; and in this opinion he certainly has the concurrence of a good many of Johnson's fellow countrymen, who have either refused to read the works or have failed after a gallant attempt.

A commonplace, I take it, is an oft-repeated truth which means nothing to the hearer of it. But for the most perfect kind of commonplace we must enlarge this definition by adding that it means nothing also to the speaker of it. Now it cannot be denied that Johnson's essays are full of commonplace in the first and narrower sense. When he came before the public as a periodical writer, he presented the world with the odd spectacle of a journalist who cared passionately for truth and nothing at all for novelty. The circulation of *The Rambler* was about five hundred copies, and the only number of it which had a great

sale was a paper by Richardson, teaching unmarried ladies
the advantages of a domestic reputation and a devout
bearing at church as effective lures for husbands. Johnson's papers often handle well-worn moral themes in general
and dogmatic language, without any effort to commend
them to the reader by particular experiences. He did not
conceal from himself the difficulty of making any impression on the wider public—'a multitude fluctuating in
pleasures or immersed in business, without time for
10 intellectual amusements.' In many passages of his works
he shows a keen appreciation of the obstacles to be surmounted before an author can capture the attention and
wield the sympathies of his readers. The chief of these
obstacles is the deep and sincere interest which every
author feels in his own work and which he imagines will
be communicated automatically to the reader. 'We are
seldom tiresome to ourselves.' Every book that can be
called a book has had one interested and excited reader.
It is surely a strange testimony to the imperfection of
20 human sympathy and the isolation of the single mind that
some books have had only one.

An author's favourite method of attack in the attempt
to cross the barrier that separates him from his reader
is the method of surprise. The writer who can startle
his public by an immediate appeal to the livelier passions
and sentiments is sure of a hearing, and can thereafter
gain attention even for the commonplace. This method
was never practised by Johnson. He despised it, for he
knew that what he had to say was no commonplace, so
30 far as he himself was concerned. Among all his discourses
on human life he utters hardly a single precept which had
not been brought home to him by living experience. The
pages of *The Rambler*, if we can read them, are aglow with
the earnestness of dear-bought conviction, and rich in
conclusions gathered not from books but from life and

suffering. It is here that the biography of the writer helps
us. If he will not come to meet us, we can go to meet
him. Any reader who acquaints himself intimately with
the records of Johnson's life, and then reads *The Rambler*,
must be very insensible if he does not find it one of the
most moving of books. It was so to Boswell, who says that
he could never read the following sentence without feeling
his frame thrill : ' I think there is some reason for question-
ing whether the body and mind are not so proportioned
that the one can bear all which can be inflicted on the 10
other ; whether virtue cannot stand its ground as long as
life, and whether a soul well principled will not be separated
sooner than subdued.'

Almost every number of *The Rambler* contains reflections and thoughts which cease to be commonplace when
the experiences that suggested them are remembered.
For more than thirty years of his mature life Johnson
was poor, often miserably poor. There are three degrees
of poverty, he said—want of riches, want of competence,
and want of necessaries. He had known them all. He 20
spoke little of this in his later years ; there is no pleasure,
he said, in narrating the annals of beggary. But his
knowledge of poverty has expressed itself more than once
in the quiet commonplaces of *The Rambler*. Again, he was
tortured by what he called indolence, but what was more
probably natural fatigue consequent upon the excessive
nervous expenditure of his bouts of hard work. And this
too finds expression in *The Rambler*. ' Indolence ', he says,
' is one of the vices from which those whom it once infects
are seldom reformed. Every other species of luxury 30
operates upon some appetite that is quickly satiated, and
requires some concurrence of art or accident which every
place will not supply ; but the desire of ease acts equally
at all hours, and the longer it is indulged is the more
increased. To do nothing is in every man's power ; we

can never want an opportunity of omitting duties.' The topics of *The Rambler* are many, but the great majority of them are drawn from the graver aspects of life, and it is when he treats of fundamental duties and inevitable sorrows, bereavement, and disease, and death, that Johnson rises to his full stature. When he ventures to emulate the tea-table morality of the *Spectator* he has not a light or happy touch. Yet his knowledge of the human mind is not only much more profound than Addison's, it is also
10 more curious and subtle. In an essay on bashfulness he first investigates its causes, and finds the chief of them in too high an opinion of our own importance. Then he applies the remedy :

' The most useful medicines are often unpleasing to the taste. Those who are oppressed by their own reputation will, perhaps, not be comforted by hearing that their cares are unnecessary. But the truth is that no man is much regarded by the rest of the world. He that considers how little he dwells upon the condition of others,
20 will learn how little the attention of others is attracted by himself. While we see multitudes passing before us, of whom, perhaps, not one appears to deserve our notice, or excite our sympathy, we should remember that we likewise are lost in the same throng ; that the eye which happens to glance upon us is turned in a moment on him that follows us, and that the utmost which we can reasonably hope or fear is, to fill a vacant hour with prattle, and be forgotten.'

This is prose that will not suffer much by comparison
30 with the best in the language. It is strange to remember, as we read some of the noblest of Johnson's sentences, that they were written in a periodical paper for the entertainment of chance readers. His essay on Revenge concludes with an appeal not often to be found in the pages of a society journal : ' Of him that hopes to be forgiven,

it is indispensably required that he forgive. It is therefore
superfluous to urge any other motive. On this great duty
eternity is suspended ; and to him that refuses to practice
it, the throne of mercy is inaccessible, and the Saviour of
the world has been born in vain.'

The passages that I have quoted from *The Rambler* are
perhaps enough to illustrate what Johnson means when
he speaks, in the last number, of his services to the English
language. 'Something, perhaps, I have added to the
elegance of its construction, and something to the harmony 10
of its cadence.' Later criticism has been inclined to say
rather that he subdued the syntax of his native tongue
to a dull mechanism, and taught it a drowsy tune. But
this is unjust. It is true that he loved balance and order,
and that the elaborate rhetorical structure of his sentences
is very ill-adapted to describe the trivial matters to which
he sometimes applies it, such as the arrival of a lady at
a country house. ' When a tiresome and vexatious journey
of four days had brought me to the house, where invitation,
regularly sent for seven years together, had at last induced 20
me to pass the summer, I was surprised, after the civilities
of my first reception, to find, instead of the leisure and
tranquillity which a rural life always promises, and, if well
conducted, might always afford, a confused wildness of
care, and a tumultuous hurry of diligence, by which every
face was clouded and every motion agitated.' In a sentence like this, the ear, which has been trained to love
completeness and symmetry, shows itself exorbitant in its
demands, and compels even the accidents of domestic life
to happen in contrasted pairs. The idle antithetical 30
members of the sentence have been compared to those
false knobs and handles which are used, for the sake of
symmetry, in a debased style of furniture. But this
occasional fault of the formal Johnsonian syntax is of
a piece with its merits. The sentence is very complex,

and when no member of it is idle, when every antithesis makes room for some new consideration, it can be packed full of meaning, so that it exhibits a subject in all its bearings, and in a few lines does the work of a chapter. When Johnson is verbose and languid, it is often because his subject is slight, and does not yield him matter enough to fill his capacious style. The syntax is still a stately organ, fitted to discourse great music, but the bellows are poor and weak. When his mind gets to work on a subject
10 that calls forth all his powers, his vigour and versatility, displayed within a narrow compass, are amazing. There is nothing new to add to his brief conclusion in the question of the second sight, which he investigated with some care during his Highland journey. ' To collect sufficient testimonies', he says, 'for the satisfaction of the public, or of ourselves, would have required more time than we could bestow. There is, against it, the seeming analogy of things confusedly seen and little understood ; and, for it, the indistinct cry of national persuasion, which may be perhaps
20 resolved at last into prejudice and tradition. I never could advance my curiosity to conviction ; but came away at last only willing to believe.'

In *The Lives of the Poets* his style reaches its maturity of vigour and ease. The author of these *Lives* is Boswell's Johnson, the brilliant talker, the king of literary society,

> Who ruled, as he thought fit,
> The universal monarchy of wit.

Yet for the light that they throw on Johnson's own character I doubt whether any of the *Lives* can compare
30 with *The Life of Richard Savage*, which was published almost twenty years before the meeting with Boswell. The character of Savage was marked, as Boswell truly observes, by profligacy, insolence, and ingratitude. But Johnson had wandered the streets with him for whole

nights together, when they could not pay for a lodging, and had taken delight in his rich and curious stores of information concerning high and low society. The *Life of Savage* is a tribute of extraordinary delicacy and beauty, paid by Johnson to his friend. Only a man of the broadest and sanest sympathies could have performed this task, which Johnson does not seem to find difficult. Towards Savage he is all tenderness and generosity, yet he does not for an instant relax his allegiance to the virtues which formed no part of his friend's character. He tells the whole truth ; yet his affection for Savage remains what he felt it to be, the most important truth of all. His morality is so entirely free from pedantry, his sense of the difficulty of virtue and the tragic force of circumstance is so keen, and his love of singularity of character is so great, that even while he points the moral of a wasted life he never comes near to the vanity of condemnation. It is abundantly clear from the facts, which he records with all the impartiality of a naturalist, that Savage, besides being hopelessly self-indulgent and dissolute, was violently egotistic, overbearing, and treacherous to his friends. Johnson's verdict on these faults is given in the closing sentences of the *Life* : ' The insolence and resentment of which he is accused were not easily to be avoided by a great mind, irritated by perpetual hardships, and constrained hourly to return the spurns of contempt and repress the insolence of prosperity ; and vanity surely may be readily pardoned in him, to whom life afforded no other comforts than barren praises and the consciousness of deserving them. Those are no proper judges of his conduct, who have slumbered away their time on the down of plenty ; nor will any wise man easily presume to say, " Had I been in Savage's condition, I should have lived or written better than Savage." '

If we try to picture Johnson in his most characteristic

attitude we usually see him sitting on that throne of human felicity, a chair in a tavern, and roaring down opposition. It was thus that Boswell knew him best, and though the same record exhibits him in many other aspects, yet the predominant impression persists. So Johnson has come to be regarded as a kind of Chairman to humanity, whose business it is to cry ' Order, Order,' an embodiment of corporate tradition and the settled wisdom of the ages.

10   Yet we may think of him, if we like, in a less public fashion, as a man full of impulse and whim, quaint in humour, passionate in feeling, warm in imagination, and, above all, original. You can never predict what Johnson will say when his opinion is challenged. Doubtless he loved paradox and argument, but he was no dialectician, and behind the play of talk his fancies and tastes were intensely individual. He disliked all talk that dealt with historical facts, especially the facts of Roman history. He never, while he lived, desired to hear of the Punic War.
20 Others besides Johnson have been distressed and fatigued by talk that is merely an exercise of memory. But his method of escape was all his own. When Mrs. Thrale asked his opinion of the conversational powers of Charles James Fox, ' He talked to me at club one day ', said Johnson, ' concerning Catiline's conspiracy—so I withdrew my attention, and thought about Tom Thumb.'

Johnson is famous for his good sense and sound judgement, but his good sense abounds in surprises. There is a delightful touch of surprise in his comparison of a ship
30 to a jail. ' No man will be a sailor who has contrivance enough to get himself into a jail ; for being in a ship is being in a jail, with the chance of being drowned.' And again, ' A man in jail has more room, better food, and commonly better company.' The same dislike of the sea expresses itself in a paper of *The Rambler* which discusses

the possibility of varying the monotony of pastoral poetry by introducing marine subjects. But unfortunately the sea has less variety than the land. ' To all the inland inhabitants of every region, the sea is only known as an immense diffusion of waters, over which men pass from one country to another, and in which life is frequently lost.'

Wherever you open the pages of Johnson's works you will find general truths sincerely and vigorously expressed, but behind the brave array of dogma you will find everywhere the strongest marks of an individual mind, and the charm and colour of personal predilections. The Romantic writers must not be allowed the credit of inventing the personal note in literature. What they invented was not themselves, but a certain sentimental way of regarding themselves. Johnson despised all such sentiment. ' When a butcher tells you,' he said, ' that his heart bleeds for his country, he has in fact no uneasy feeling.' Rousseau is not more individual in his cultivation of sentiment than Johnson in his dislike of it. He carried this dislike to strange extremes, so that all gesticulation and expression of the emotions became suspect to him. Of the preaching of Dr. Isaac Watts he says, ' He did not endeavour to assist his eloquence by any gesticulations ; for, as no corporeal actions have any correspondence with theological truth, he did not see how they could enforce it.' Perhaps the best example of this fixed distaste for demonstrative emotion may be found in his contempt for the actor's profession. It is dangerous to quarrel with Boswell, but it seems to me impossible to accept his suggestion that Johnson's opinions concerning stage-players had their origin in jealousy of the success of Garrick. Such jealousy is utterly unlike all that we know of Johnson. On the other hand, a hatred of show and a fierce resentment at the response of his own feelings to cunningly simulated passion are exactly what we should expect in him. The passages in which he

has expressed himself on this matter are too many and too various to be attributed to a gust of personal ill-feeling. One of the most delightful of them occurs in his notes on the character of Bottom in *A Midsummer Night's Dream.* ' Bottom ', he says, ' seems to have been bred in a tiring-room. He is for engrossing every part, and would exclude his inferiors from all possibility of distinction.' Again, ' Bottom discovers a true genius for the stage by his solicitude for propriety of dress, and his deliberation
10 which beard to choose among many beards, all unnatural.'

The sonorous and ponderous rotundity of Johnson's style, and the unfailing respect that he pays to law and decorum, have partly concealed from view the wilfulness of his native temper. Obedience to law imposed from without can never be the soul of a man or of a writer. It is the converted rebels who give power to the arm of government. If there has ever been a writer of a sober, slow and conforming temper, who has left memorable work behind him, it will be found, I think, that for the
20 greater part of his life he acted as a poor mechanical drudge in the service of his own youthful enthusiasm, and painfully filled out the schemes which were conceived in a happier time. All enduring literary work is the offspring of intense excitement. Johnson did most of his reading piecemeal, in a fever of agitation. If any man praised a book in his presence, he was sure to ask, ' Did you read it through ? ' If the answer was in the affirmative, he did not seem willing to believe it. He very seldom read a book from beginning to end ; his writing, moreover,
30 was done at high speed, and often at a great heat of imagination. Some writers use general statements as a mask to conceal ignorance and emptiness : Johnson prefers them because they lend smoothness and decency to passion. He states only his conclusions ; but the premises, although they are not given, are vividly present

to his mind. When it becomes necessary, as a guarantee of sincerity and knowledge, to exhibit in full all that is implied in a general statement, he reverses his favourite method, and permits his imagination to expatiate on his material with all the visionary activity of poetry. His review of Soame Jenyns's *Free Enquiry into the Nature and Origin of Evil* furnishes a splendid instance of this imaginative power, which expands an abstract proposition into all its detailed consequences. Soame Jenyns was a gentleman with a taste for metaphysic, who had offered 10 some conjectures, in the glib optimistic vein of Pope, towards the explanation of failure and suffering. In the course of his essays he touches, with a light hand, on the possible compensations and advantages of pain and poverty. In order to demonstrate that all partial evil is universal good he constructs an airy hierarchy, or graduated scale of imaginary beings, each rank of whom he supposes to derive benefit from the pains of those who inhabit a lower grade. Johnson's piety and humility, his profound sense of the reality of human suffering and the weakness of human 20 faculty, were outraged by this fantastic philosophy. ' To these speculations', he says, ' humanity is unequal.' In a passage of relentless satire Soame Jenyns is introduced, for the first time, to the meaning of his own hypothesis. ' He imagines ', says Johnson, ' that as we have not only animals for food, but choose some for our own diversion, the same privilege may be allowed to some beings above us, *who may deceive, torment, or destroy us for the ends only of their own pleasure and utility.* This he again finds impossible to be conceived, *but that impossibility lessens* 30 *not the probability of the conjecture, which by analogy is so strongly confirmed.*

' I cannot resist the temptation of contemplating this analogy, which, I think, he might have carried further, very much to the advantage of his argument. He might

have shown that *these hunters, whose game is man,* have
many sports analogous to our own. As we drown whelps
and kittens, they amuse themselves now and then with
sinking a ship, and stand round the fields of Blenheim
or the walls of Prague, as we encircle a cock-pit. As we
shoot a bird flying, they take a man in the midst of his
business or pleasure, and knock him down with an apoplexy.
Some of them, perhaps, are virtuosi, and delight in the
operations of an asthma, as a human philosopher in the
10 effects of an air-pump. To swell a man with a tympany
is as good sport as to blow a frog. Many a merry bout have
these frolic beings at the vicissitudes of an ague, and good
sport it is to see a man tumble with epilepsy, and revive
and tumble again, and all this he knows not why. As they
are wiser and more powerful than we, they have more
exquisite diversions, for we have no way of procuring
any sport so brisk and so lasting as the paroxysms of the
gout and the stone, which undoubtedly must make high
mirth, especially if the play be a little diversified with the
20 blunders and puzzles of the blind and deaf. We know not
how far their sphere of observation may extend. Perhaps
now and then a merry being may place himself in such
a situation as to enjoy at once all the varieties of an
epidemical disease, or amuse his leisure with the tossings
and contortions of every possible pain exhibited together.

' One sport the merry malice of these beings has found
means of enjoying to which we have nothing equal or
similar. They now and then catch a mortal proud of his
parts, and flattered either by the submission of those
30 who court his kindness or the notice of those who suffer
him to court theirs. A head thus prepared for the reception of false opinions and the projection of vain designs
they easily fill with idle notions, till in time they make their
plaything an author : their first diversion commonly begins
with an ode or an epistle, then rises perhaps to a political

irony, and is at last brought to its height by a treatise of
philosophy. Then begins the poor animal to entangle
himself in sophisms and flounder in absurdity, to talk
confidently of the scale of being and to give solutions which
himself confesses impossible to be understood. Sometimes,
however, it happens that their pleasure is without much
mischief. The author feels no pain, but while they are
wondering at the extravagance of his opinion, and pointing
him out to one another as a new example of human folly
he is enjoying his own applause and that of his com- 10
panions, and perhaps is elevated with the hope of standing
at the head of a new sect.

'Many of the books which now crowd the world may
be justly suspected to be written for the sake of some
invisible order of beings—for surely they are of no use
to any of the corporeal inhabitants of the world. . . .
The only reason why we should contemplate Evil is,
that we may bear it better; and I am afraid nothing is
much more placidly endured for the sake of making others
sport.'   20

Johnson, it may be remarked, does not answer Soame
Jenyns's argument; he concentrates on it the heat of
his imagination, and it shrivels under the glow. He felt
no respect for a structure of theory, however ingenious
and elaborate, which is built up from facts imperfectly
realized. 'Life', he says, 'must be seen before it can be
known.' Because he had seen much of life, his last and
greatest work, *The Lives of the Most Eminent English
Poets*, is more than a collection of facts: it is a book of
wisdom and experience, a treatise on the conduct of life, 30
a commentary on human destiny.

Those *Lives* will never lose their authoritative value
as a record. The biographer must often consult them
for their facts. The student of Johnson will consult
them quite as often for the light that they throw on their

author, who moves among *the* English poets easily and freely, enjoying the society of his peers, praising them without timidity, judging them without superstition, yet ready at all times with those human allowances which are more likely to be kept in mind by a man's intimates than by an indifferent posterity. When Johnson undertook the *Lives* he was almost seventy years of age ; he had long been familiar with his subject, and he wrote from a full mind, rapidly and confidently. He spent little time on
10 research. When Boswell tried to introduce him to Lord Marchmont, who had a store of anecdotes concerning Pope, he at first refused the trouble of hearing them. ' I suppose, Sir,' said Mrs. Thrale, with something of the severity of a governess, ' Mr. Boswell thought, that as you are to write Pope's *Life*, you would wish to know about him.' Johnson accepted the reproof, though he might very well have replied that he knew more than was necessary for his purpose. An even better instance of his indifference may be found in his criticism of Congreve. Congreve's
20 dramatic works are not bulky, and were doubtless to be found in any well-appointed drawing-room. But Johnson would not rise from his desk. ' Of Congreve's plays ', he says, ' I cannot speak distinctly ; for since I inspected them many years have passed ; but what remains upon my memory is, that his characters are commonly fictitious and artificial, with very little of nature and not much of life.' Then follows an admirable critical summary of Congreve's peculiar merits in comedy.

This magnanimous carelessness with regard to detail
30 helped rather than hindered the breadth and justice of Johnson's scheme. There are many modern biographies and histories, full of carefully authenticated fact, which afflict the reader with a weight of indigestion. The author has no right to his facts, no ownership in them. They have flitted through his mind on a calm five minutes'

passage from the note-book to the immortality of the printed page. But no man can hope to make much impression on a reader with facts which he has not thought it worth his own while to remember. Every considerable book, in literature or science, is an engine whereby mind operates on mind. It is an ignorant worship of Science which treats it as residing in books, and reduces the mind to a mechanism of transfer. The measure of an author's power would be best found in the book which he should sit down to write the day after his library was burnt to the ground.

The *Lives of the Poets* has not a few of the qualities of such a book. It is broadly conceived and written, it has a firm grasp of essentials, the portraits are lifelike, and the judgements, on the whole, wonderfully fair. There has been much extravagant talk among Romantic critics of Johnson's prejudices, and even of his incapacity as a judge of poetry. Time will avenge him on these critics ; and Time has begun to do its work. The minor poets of our own day may well be glad that Johnson is not alive among them.

His occasional errors cannot be concealed ; they are known to every schoolboy. Sometimes he allows his own matured and carefully considered views on certain general literary questions to interfere with the impartial examination of a particular poem. He disliked irregular metres and fortuitous schemes of rhyme. He held the pastoral convention in poetry to be artificial, frigid, and over-worn. These opinions and tastes led him into his notorious verdict on *Lycidas*. And yet, when the noise of the shouting shall have died away, it may be questioned whether most of the points attacked by Johnson would ever be chosen by admirers of the poem for special commendation. Is there nothing artificial and far-fetched about the satyrs and the fauns with cloven heel ? Is the ceremonial procession of Triton, Camus, and St. Peter an example of Milton's imagination at its best ? In short, does the beauty and wonder of the poem derive from the allegorical scheme to which Johnson objected ? But I am almost frightened at my own temerity, and must be content to leave the question unanswered.

There were certain of the English poets whom Johnson, it is plain, disliked, even while he admired their work. His account of them is inevitably tinged by this dislike ; yet his native generosity and justice never shine out more brightly than in the praises that he gives them. He disliked Milton ; and no one has ever written a more whole-hearted eulogy of *Paradise Lost.* Unless I am deceived, he disliked many things in the character of Addison, yet any one who would praise Addison nobly and truly will find himself compelled to echo Johnson's praises. A more profound difference of feeling separated him from Swift. He excuses himself from writing a fuller account of Swift's life, on the ground that the task had already been performed by Dr. Hawkesworth. But Hawkesworth's *Life* is a mere piece of book-making, and it seems likely that Johnson was glad to be saved from a duty that had no attractions for him. The contrast between himself and Swift may be best expressed in their own words : ' I heartily hate and detest that animal called man,' said Swift, ' although I heartily love John, Peter, Thomas, and so forth.' Johnson's attitude was the reverse of this. He used to say that the world was well constructed, but that the particular people disgraced the elegance and beauty of the general fabric. Yet it was he, not the hearty lover of ' John, Peter, Thomas, and so forth ', who had the deeper sense of the tie that binds man to man. That men should dare to hate each other in a world where they suffer the like trials and await the same doom was hardly conceivable to Johnson. That a man should dare to stand

aloof from his kind and condemn them was a higher pitch
of arrogance, destined to end in that tempest of madness
and hate which is the Fourth Book of *Gulliver's Travels*.

Lastly, it cannot be denied that Johnson did scant
justice to Gray ; although here, again, his praise of the
Elegy could hardly be bettered. The causes of this imper-
fect sympathy are easy to understand. Gray was a recluse
poet, shy, sensitive, dainty, who brooded on his own
feelings and guarded his own genius from contact with the
rough world. ' He had a notion,' says Johnson, ' not very
peculiar, that he could not write but at certain times, or
at happy moments ; a fantastic foppery, to which my
kindness for a man of learning and virtue wishes him to have
been superior.' Surely this impatience will seem only
natural to those who remember the story of Johnson's
life. He had lived for thirty years, and had supported
others, solely by the labours of his pen. The pay he received
was often wretchedly small. Fifteen guineas was the price
of the copyright of the *Life of Savage.* He was driven from
task to task, compelled to supply the booksellers with
what they demanded, prefaces, translations, or sermons at
a guinea a piece. In spite of sickness and lassitude and intense disinclination, the day's work had to be done, and
when work did not come to hand, it had to be sought
and solicited. It is not easy for us to imagine the con-
ditions of literature in London when Johnson first came
there, and for many years after,—the crowds of miserable
authors, poor, servile, jealous, and venal. Immersed in this
society he laboured for years. The laws that he imposed
on his drudgery were never broken. He made no personal
attacks on others, and answered none on himself. He never
complied with temporary curiosity, nor enabled his readers
to discuss the topic of the day. He never degraded virtue
by the meanness of dedication. There was nothing in his
writings to disclaim and nothing to regret, for he always

thought it the duty of an anonymous author to write as if he expected to be hereafter known. When at last he was known, there was still no escape from hack-work and the necessities of the day. The books which he has added to the English Classics were written for bread—the *Dictionary*, the periodical papers, *Rasselas*, the Preface and Notes to Shakespeare (which will some day be recognized for what they are, the best and most luminous of eighteenth century commentaries on Shakespeare's drama), and the *Lives of the Poets*.

This is the greatness of Johnson, that he is greater than his works. He thought of himself as a man, not as an author; and of literature as a means, not as an end in itself. Duties and friendships and charities were more to him than fame and honour. The breadth and humanity of temper which sometimes caused him to depreciate the importance of literature, have left their mark on his books. There are some authors who exhaust themselves in the effort to endow posterity, and distil all their virtue in a book. Yet their masterpieces have something inhuman about them, like those jewelled idols, the work of men's hands, which are worshipped by the sacrifice of man's flesh and blood. There is more of comfort and dignity in the view of literature to which Johnson has given large utterance : ' Books without the knowledge of life are useless ; for what should books teach but the art of living ? '

Selections from

J O H N S O N ' S

Writings

THE

VANITY

O F

HUMAN WISHES.

THE

Tenth Satire of *Juvenal*,

IMITATED

By *SAMUEL JOHNSON.*

LONDON:

Printed for R. Dodsley at Tully's Head in Pall-Mall, and Sold by M. Cooper in Pater-nofter Row.

M.DCC.XLIX.

THE

VANITY

OF

HUMAN WISHES.

LET Observation with extensive View,
Survey Mankind, from *China* to *Peru*;
Remark each anxious Toil, each eager Strife,
And watch the busy Scenes of crouded Life;
Then say how Hope and Fear, Desire and Hate,
O'erspread with Snares the clouded Maze of Fate,
Where wav'ring Man, betray'd by vent'rous Pride,
To tread the dreary Paths without a Guide;
As treach'rous Phantoms in the Mist delude,
Shuns fancied Ills, or chases airy Good.   10
How rarely Reason guides the stubborn Choice,
Rules the bold Hand, or prompts the suppliant Voice,
How Nations sink, by darling Schemes oppress'd,
When Vengeance listens to the Fool's Request.
Fate wings with ev'ry Wish th' afflictive Dart,
Each Gift of Nature, and each Grace of Art,
With fatal Heat impetuous Courage glows,
With fatal Sweetness Elocution flows,
Impeachment stops the Speaker's pow'rful Breath,
And restless Fire precipitates on Death.   20

But scarce observ'd the Knowing and the Bold,
Fall in the gen'ral Massacre of Gold ;
Wide-wasting Pest ! that rages unconfin'd,
And crouds with Crimes the Records of Mankind,
For Gold his Sword the Hireling Ruffian draws,
For Gold the hireling Judge distorts the Laws ;
Wealth heap'd on Wealth, nor Truth nor Safety buys,
The Dangers gather as the Treasures rise.

Let Hist'ry tell, where rival Kings command,
And dubious Title shakes the madded Land,   30
When Statutes glean the Refuse of the Sword,
How much more safe the Vassal than the Lord,
Low skulks the Hind beneath the Rage of Pow'r,
And leaves the wealthy Traitor in the Tow'r,
Untouch'd his Cottage, and his Slumbers sound,
Tho' Confiscation's Vulturs hover round.

The needy Traveller, serene and gay,
Walks the wild Heath, and sings his Toil away.
Does Envy seize thee ? crush th' upbraiding Joy,
Encrease his Riches and his Peace destroy,   40
Now fears in dire Vicissitude invade,
The rustling Brake alarms, and quiv'ring Shade,
Nor Light nor Darkness bring his Pain Relief,
One shews the Plunder, and one hides the Thief.

Yet still one gen'ral Cry the Skies assails,
And Gain and Grandeur load the tainted Gales ;
Few know the toiling Statesman's Fear or Care,
Th' insidious Rival and the gaping Heir.

Once more, *Democritus*, arise on Earth,
With chearful Wisdom and instructive Mirth,   50
See motley Life in modern Trappings dress'd,
And feed with varied Fools th' eternal Jest :

Thou who could'st laugh where Want enchain'd Caprice,
Toil crush'd Conceit, and Man was of a Piece ;
Where Wealth unlov'd without a Mourner dy'd ;
And scarce a Sycophant was fed by Pride ;
Where ne'er was known the Form of mock Debate,
Or seen a new-made Mayor's unwieldy State ;
Where change of Fav'rites made no Change of Laws,
And Senates heard before they judg'd a Cause ;   60
How would'st thou shake at *Britain's* modish Tribe,
Dart the quick Taunt, and edge the piercing Gibe !
Attentive Truth and Nature to descry,
And pierce each Scene with Philosophic Eye.
To thee were solemn Toys or empty Shew,
The Robes of Pleasure and the Veils of Woe :
All aid the Farce, and all thy Mirth maintain,
Whose Joys are causeless, or whose Griefs are vain.

Such was the Scorn that fill'd the Sage's Mind,
Renew'd at ev'ry Glance on Humankind ;   70
How just that Scorn ere yet thy Voice declare,
Search ev'ry State, and canvass ev'ry Pray'r.

Unnumber'd Suppliants croud Preferment's Gate,
Athirst for Wealth, and burning to be great ;
Delusive Fortune hears th' incessant Call,
They mount, they shine, evaporate, and fall.
On ev'ry Stage the Foes of Peace attend,
Hate dogs their Flight, and Insult mocks their End.
Love ends with Hope, the sinking Statesman's Door
Pours in the Morning Worshipper no more ;   80
For growing Names the weekly Scribbler lies,
To growing Wealth the Dedicator flies.
From ev'ry Room descends the painted Face,
That hung the bright *Palladium* of the Place,
And smoak'd in Kitchens, or in Auctions sold,

To better Features yields the Frame of Gold ;
For now no more we trace in ev'ry Line
Heroic Worth, Benevolence Divine :
The Form distorted justifies the Fall,
And Detestation rids th' indignant Wall.   90

But will not *Britain* hear the last Appeal,
Sign her Foe's Doom, or guard her Fav'rite's Zeal ;
Through Freedom's Sons no more Remonstrance rings,
Degrading Nobles and controulling Kings ;
Our supple Tribes repress their Patriot Throats,
And ask no Questions but the Price of Votes ;
With Weekly Libels and Septennial Ale,
Their Wish is full to riot and to rail.

In full-blown Dignity, see *Wolsey* stand,
Law in his Voice, and Fortune in his Hand :   100
To him the Church, the Realm, their Pow'rs consign,
Thro' him the Rays of regal Bounty shine,
Turn'd by his Nod the Stream of Honour flows,
His Smile alone Security bestows :
Still to new Heights his restless Wishes tow'r,
Claim leads to Claim, and Pow'r advances Pow'r :
Till Conquest unresisted ceas'd to please,
And Rights submitted, left him none to seize.
At length his Sov'reign frowns—the Train of State
Mark the keen Glance, and watch the Sign to hate.   110
Wher-e'er he turns he meets a Stranger's eye,
His Suppliants scorn him, and his Followers fly ;
At once is lost the Pride of aweful State,
The golden Canopy, the glitt'ring Plate,
The regal Palace, the luxurious Board,
The liv'ried Army, and the menial Lord.
With Age, with Cares, with Maladies oppress'd,
He seeks the Refuge of Monastic Rest.

Grief aids Disease, remember'd Folly stings,
And his last Sighs reproach the Faith of Kings.   120

Speak thou, whose Thoughts at humble Peace repine,
Shall *Wolsey's* Wealth, with *Wolsey's* End be thine?
Or liv'st thou now, with safer Pride content,
The richest Landlord on the banks of *Trent*?
For why did *Wolsey* near the Steeps of Fate,
On weak Foundations raise th' enormous Weight?
Why but to sink beneath Misfortune's Blow,
With louder Ruin to the gulphs below?

What gave great *Villiers* to th' Assassin's Knife,
And fix'd Disease on *Harley's* closing Life?   130
What murder'd *Wentworth*, and what exil'd *Hyde*,
By Kings protected and to Kings ally'd?
What but their Wish indulg'd in Courts to shine,
And Pow'r too great to keep or to resign?

When first the College Rolls receive his Name,
The young Enthusiast quits his Ease for Fame;
Thro' all his Veins the Fever of Renown
Burns from the strong Contagion of the Gown;
O'er *Bodley's* Dome his future Labours spread
And *Bacon's* Mansion trembles o'er his Head;   140
Are these thy Views? proceed, illustrious Youth,
And Virtue guard thee to the Throne of Truth.
Yet should thy Soul indulge the gen'rous Heat
Till captive Science yields her last Retreat;
Should Reason guide thee with her brightest Ray,
And pour on misty Doubt resistless Day;
Should no false Kindness lure to loose Delight,
Nor Praise relax, nor Difficulty fright;
Should tempting Novelty thy Cell refrain,
And Sloth effuse her opiate Fumes in Vain: 150

Should Beauty blunt on Fops her fatal Dart,
Nor claim the triumph of a letter'd Heart;
Should no Disease thy torpid Veins invade,
Nor Melancholy's Phantoms haunt thy shade;
Yet hope not Life from Grief or Danger free,
Nor think the Doom of Man revers'd for thee.
Deign on the passing World to turn thine Eyes,
And pause awhile from Letters to be wise;
There mark what Ills the Scholar's Life assail,
Toil, Envy, Want, the Patron, and the Jail.   160
See Nations slowly wise, and meanly just,
To buried Merit raise the tardy Bust.
If Dreams yet flatter, once again attend,
Hear *Lydiat's* Life, and *Galileo's* End.

Nor deem, when Learning her last Prize bestows
The glitt'ring Eminence exempt from Foes;
See when the Vulgar 'scape, despis'd or aw'd,
Rebellion's vengeful Talons seize on *Laud*.
From meaner Minds, tho' smaller Fines content
The plunder'd Palace or sequester'd Rent;   170
Mark'd out by dang'rous Parts he meets the Shock,
And fatal Learning leads him to the Block:
Around his Tomb let Art and Genius weep,
But hear his Death, ye Blockheads, hear and sleep.

The festal Blazes, the triumphal Show,
The ravish'd Standard, and the captive Foe,
The Senate's Thanks, the Gazette's pompous Tale,
With Force resistless o'er the Brave prevail.
Such Bribes the rapid *Greek* o'er *Asia* whirl'd,
For such the steady *Romans* shook the World;   180
For such in distant Lands the *Britons* shine,
And stain with Blood the *Danube* or the *Rhine*;

This Pow'r has Praise, that Virtue scarce can warm,
Till Fame supplies the universal Charm.
Yet Reason frowns on War's unequal Game,
Where wasted Nations raise a single Name,
And mortgag'd States their Grandsires' Wreaths regret,
From Age to Age in everlasting Debt ;
Wreaths which at last the dear-bought Right convey
To rust on Medals, or on Stones decay.   190

   On what Foundation stands the Warrior's Pride ?
How just his Hopes let *Swedish Charles* decide ;
A Frame of Adamant, a Soul of Fire,
No Dangers fright him and no Labours tire ;
O'er Love, o'er Fear, extends his wide Domain,
Unconquer'd Lord of Pleasure and of Pain ;
No Joys to him pacific Scepters yield,
War sounds the Trump, he rushes to the Field ;
Behold surrounding Kings their pow'rs combine,
And One capitulate, and One resign :   200
Peace courts his Hand, but spreads her Charms in vain ;
' Think Nothing gain'd ', he cries, ' till nought remain,
' On *Moscow*'s Walls till *Gothic* standards fly,
' And all be Mine beneath the Polar Sky.'
The March begins in Military State,
And Nations on his Eye suspended wait ;
Stern Famine guards the solitary Coast,
And Winter barricades the Realms of Frost ;
He comes, nor Want nor Cold his Course delay ;—
Hide, blushing Glory, hide *Pultowa's* day :   210
The vanquish'd Hero leaves his broken Bands,
And shows his Miseries in distant Lands ;
Condemn'd a needy Supplicant to wait,
While Ladies interpose, and Slaves debate.
But did not Chance at length her Error mend ?
Did no subverted Empire mark his End ?

Did rival Monarchs give the fatal Wound?
Or hostile Millions press him to the Ground?
His Fall was destin'd to a barren Strand,
A petty Fortress, and a dubious Hand;   220
He left the Name, at which the World grew pale,
To point a Moral, or adorn a Tale.

All Times their Scenes of pompous Woes afford,
From *Persia's* Tyrant to *Bavaria's* Lord.
In gay Hostility, and barb'rous Pride,
With half Mankind embattled at his Side,
Great *Xerxes* comes to seize the certain prey,
And starves exhausted Regions in his Way;
Attendant Flatt'ry counts his Myriads o'er,
Till counted Myriads soothe his Pride no more;   230
Fresh praise is try'd till Madness fires his Mind,
The Waves he lashes, and enchains the Wind;
New Pow'rs are claim'd, new Pow'rs are still bestow'd,
Till rude Resistance lops the spreading God;
The daring *Greeks* deride the Martial Shew,
And heap their Vallies with the gaudy Foe;
Th' insulted Sea with humbler Thoughts he gains,
A single Skiff to speed his Flight remains;
Th' encumber'd Oar scarce leaves the dreaded Coast
Thro' purple Billows and a floating Host.   240

The bold *Bavarian*, in a luckless Hour,
Tries the dread Summits of *Cesarean* pow'r,
With unexpected Legions bursts away,
And sees defenceless Realms receive his Sway;
Short Sway! fair *Austria* spreads her mournful Charms,
The Queen, the Beauty, sets the World in Arms;
From Hill to Hill the Beacon's rousing Blaze
Spreads wide the Hope of Plunder and of Praise;

The fierce *Croatian*, and the wild *Hussar*,
With all the Sons of Ravage, croud the War;   250
The baffled Prince in Honour's flatt'ring Bloom
Of hasty Greatness finds the fatal Doom,
His Foes' Derision and his Subjects' Blame,
And steals to Death from Anguish and from Shame.

' Enlarge my Life with Multitude of Days,'
In Health, in Sickness, thus the Suppliant prays:
Hides from himself his State, and shuns to know,
That Life protracted is protracted Woe.
Time hovers o'er, impatient to destroy,
And shuts up all the Passages of Joy: 260
In vain their Gifts the bounteous Seasons pour,
The Fruit Autumnal, and the Vernal Flow'r,
With listless Eyes the Dotard views the Store,
He views, and wonders that they please no more;
Now pall the tasteless Meats, and joyless Wines,
And Luxury with Sighs her Slave resigns.
Approach, ye Minstrels, try the soothing Strain,
Diffuse the tuneful Lenitives of Pain:
No sounds alas would touch th' impervious Ear,
Though dancing Mountains witness'd *Orpheus* near;   270
Nor Lute nor Lyre his feeble pow'rs attend,
Nor sweeter Music of a virtuous Friend,
But everlasting Dictates croud his Tongue,
Perversely grave, or positively wrong;
The still returning Tale, and ling'ring Jest,
Perplex the fawning Niece and pamper'd Guest,
While growing Hopes scarce awe the gath'ring Sneer,
And scarce a Legacy can bribe to hear;
The watchful Guests still hint the last Offence,
The Daughter's Petulance, the son's Expence,   280
Improve his heady Rage with treach'rous Skill,
And mould his Passions till they make his Will.

G 2

Unnumber'd Maladies his Joints invade,
Lay Siege to Life and press the dire Blockade ;
But unextinguish'd Av'rice still remains,
And dreaded Losses aggravate his Pains :
He turns, with anxious Heart and crippled Hands,
His Bonds of Debt, and Mortgages of Lands ;
Or views his Coffers with suspicious Eyes,
Unlocks his Gold, and counts it till he dies.   290

But grant, the Virtues of a temp'rate Prime
Bless with an Age exempt from Scorn or Crime ;
An Age that melts with unperceiv'd Decay,
And glides in modest Innocence away ;
Whose peaceful Day Benevolence endears,
Whose Night congratulating Conscience cheers ;
The gen'ral Fav'rite as the gen'ral Friend :
Such Age there is, and who shall wish its End ?

Yet ev'n on this her Load Misfortune flings,
To press the weary Minutes' flagging Wings ;   300
New Sorrow rises as the Day returns,
A Sister sickens, or a Daughter mourns.
Now Kindred Merit fills the sable Bier,
Now lacerated Friendship claims a Tear.
Year chases Year, Decay pursues Decay,
Still drops some Joy from with'ring Life away ;
New Forms arise, and diff'rent views Engage,
Superfluous lags the Vet'ran on the Stage,
Till pitying Nature signs the last Release,
And bids afflicted Worth retire to Peace.   310

But few there are whom Hours like these await,
Who set unclouded in the Gulphs of Fate.
From *Lydia's* Monarch should the Search descend,
By *Solon* caution'd to regard his End,

In Life's last Scene what Prodigies surprise,
Fears of the Brave, and Follies of the Wise !
From *Marlb'rough's* Eyes the Streams of Dotage flow,
And *Swift* expires a Driv'ler and a Show.

The teeming Mother, anxious for her Race,
Begs for each Birth the Fortune of a Face ;   320
Yet *Vane* could tell what Ills from Beauty spring ;
And *Sedley* curs'd the Form that pleas'd a King.
Ye Nymphs of rosy Lips and radiant Eyes,
Whom Pleasure keeps too busy to be wise,
Whom Joys with soft Varieties invite,
By Day the Frolic, and the Dance by Night ;
Who frown with Vanity, who smile with Art,
And ask the latest Fashion of the Heart,
What Care, what Rules your heedless Charms shall save,
Each Nymph your Rival, and each Youth your Slave ?   330
Against your Fame with Fondness Hate combines,
The Rival batters, and the Lover mines.
With distant Voice neglected Virtue calls,
Less heard, and less, the faint Remonstrance falls ;
Tir'd with Contempt, she quits the slipp'ry Reign,
And Pride and Prudence take her Seat in vain.
In croud at once, where none the Pass defend,
The harmless Freedom, and the private Friend.
The Guardians yield, by Force superior ply'd ;
By Int'rest, Prudence ; and by Fiatt'ry, Pride.   340
Here Beauty falls betray'd, despis'd, distress'd,
And hissing Infamy proclaims the rest.

Where then shall Hope and Fear their Objects find ?
Must dull Suspence corrupt the stagnant Mind ?
Must helpless Man, in Ignorance sedate,
Roll darkling down the Torrent of his Fate ?

Must no Dislike alarm, no Wishes rise,
No Cries attempt the Mercies of the skies ?
Enquirer, cease, Petitions yet remain,
Which Heav'n may hear, nor deem Religion vain.   350
Still raise for Good the supplicating Voice,
But leave to Heav'n the Measure and the Choice.
Safe in his Pow'r, whose Eyes discern afar
The secret Ambush of a specious Pray'r.
Implore his Aid, in his Decisions rest,
Secure, whate'er he gives, he gives the best.
Yet when the Sense of sacred Presence fires,
And strong Devotion to the Skies aspires,
Pour forth thy Fervours for a healthful Mind,
Obedient Passions, and a Will resign'd ;   360
For Love, which scarce collective Man can fill ;
For Patience, Sov'reign o'er transmuted ill ;
For Faith, that panting for a happier Seat,
Counts Death kind Nature's Signal of Retreat.
These Goods for Man the Laws of Heav'n ordain,
These Goods he grants, who grants the Pow'r to gain ;
With these celestial Wisdom calms the Mind,
And makes the Happiness she does not find.

FINIS.

ON THE DEATH OF

Mr. ROBERT LEVET,

A PRACTISER IN PHYSIC

Written in 1782.

CONDEMN'D to Hope's delusive mine,
  As on we toil from day to day,
By sudden blasts, or slow decline,
  Our social comforts drop away.

Well try'd through many a varying year,
  See Levet to the grave descend,
Officious, innocent, sincere,
  Of every friendless name the friend.

Yet still he fills affection's eye,
  Obscurely wise and coarsely kind;   10
Nor letter'd arrogance deny
  Thy praise to merit unrefin'd.

When fainting nature call'd for aid,
  And hovering death prepar'd the blow,
His vigorous remedy display'd
  The power of art without the show.

In misery's darkest cavern known,
  His useful care was ever nigh,
Where hopeless anguish pour'd his groan,
  And lonely want retir'd to die.   20

No summons mock'd by chill delay,
  No petty gain disdain'd by pride;
The modest wants of every day
  The toil of every day supply'd.

His virtues walk'd their narrow round,
  Nor made a pause, nor left a void:
And sure th' Eternal master found
  The single talent well employ'd.

The busy day—the peaceful night,
  Unfelt, uncounted, glided by;   30
His frame was firm—his powers were bright,
  Tho' now his *eightieth* year was nigh.

Then with no fiery throbbing pain,
  No cold gradations of decay,
Death broke at once the vital chain,
  And freed his soul the nearest way.

From THE RAMBLER

*Published every Tuesday and Saturday from 20 March, 1750
to 14 March, 1752.*

NUMB. 19. TUESDAY, *May* 22, 1750.

*Dum te causidicum, dum te modo rhetora fingis,
  Et non decernis, Taure, quid esse velis,
Peleos & Priami transit, vel Nestoris ætas,
  Et serum fuerat jam tibi desinere. . . .
Eja, age, rumpe moras, quo te spectabimus usque?
  Dum quid sis dubitas, jam potes esse nihil.*

MART.

To rhetoric now, and now to law inclin'd,
Uncertain where to fix thy changing mind;
Old *Priam's* age or *Nestor's* may be out,
And thou, O *Taurus*, still go on in doubt.
Come then, how long such wav'ring shall we see?
Thou may'st doubt on: thou now can'st nothing be.

F. LEWIS.

IT is never without very melancholy reflexions, that we
can observe the misconduct, or miscarriage, of those men,
who seem, by the force of understanding, or extent of
knowledge, exempted from the general frailties of human
nature, and privileged from the common infelicities of life.
Though the world is crowded with scenes of calamity, we
look upon the general mass of wretchedness with very little
regard, and fix our eyes upon the state of particular
persons, whom the eminence of their qualities marks out
from the multitude; as, in reading an account of a battle, 10
we seldom reflect on the vulgar heaps of slaughter, but
follow the hero, with our whole attention, through all the
varieties of his fortune, without a thought of the thousands
that are falling round him.

With the same kind of anxious veneration I have for many years been making observations on the life of Polyphilus, a man whom all his acquaintances have, from his first appearance in the world, feared for the quickness of his discernment, and admired for the multiplicity of his attainments, but whose progress in life, and usefulness to mankind has been hindered by the superfluity of his knowledge, and the celerity of his mind.

Polyphilus was remarkable, at the school, for surpassing
10 all his companions, without any visible application, and at the university was distinguished equally for his successful progress as well through the thorny mazes of science, as the flowery path of politer literature, without any strict confinement to hours of study, or remarkable forbearance of the common amusements of young men.

When Polyphilus was at the age, in which men usually chuse their profession, and prepare to enter into a public character, every academical eye was fixed upon him ; all were curious to inquire, what this universal genius
20 would fix upon for the employment of his life ; and no doubt was made but that he would leave all his contemporaries behind him, and mount to the highest honours of that class, in which he should inlist himself, without those delays and pauses which must be endured by meaner abilities.

Polyphilus, though by no means insolent or assuming, had been sufficiently encouraged, by uninterrupted success, to place great confidence in his own parts ; and was not below his companions in the indulgence of his hopes, and
30 expectation of the astonishment with which the world would be struck, when first his lustre should break out upon it ; nor could he forbear (for whom does not constant flattery intoxicate ?) to join sometimes in the mirth of his friends, at the sudden disappearance of those, who, having shone awhile, and drawn the eyes of the public upon their

feeble radiance, were now doomed to fade away before him.

It is natural for a man to catch advantageous notions of the condition which those, with whom he converses, are striving to attain. Polyphilus, in a ramble to London, fell accidentally among the physicians, and was so much pleased with the prospect of turning philosophy to profit, and so highly delighted with a new theory of fevers which darted into his imagination, and which, after having considered it a few hours, he found himself able to maintain against all the advocates for the ancient system, that he resolved to apply himself to anatomy, botany, and chemistry, and to leave no part unconquered either of the animal, mineral, or vegetable kingdoms.

He therefore read authors, constructed systems, and tried experiments ; but unhappily, as he was going to see a new plant in flower at Chelsea, he met, in crossing Westminster to take water, the chancellor's coach ; he had the curiosity to follow him into the hall, where a remarkable cause happened to be tryed, and found himself able to produce so many arguments, which the lawyers had omitted on both sides, that he determined to quit physic for a profession, in which he found it would be so easy to excel, and which promised higher honours, and larger profits, without melancholy attendance upon misery, mean submission to peevishness, and continual interruption of rest and pleasure.

He immediately took chambers in the Temple, bought a common-place-book, and confined himself for some months to the perusal of the statutes, year-books, pleadings, and reports ; he was a constant hearer of the courts, and began to put cases with reasonable accuracy. But he soon discovered, by considering the fortune of lawyers, that preferment was not to be got by acuteness, learning, and eloquence. He was perplexed by the absurdities of attorneys, and misrepresentations made by his clients of

their own causes, by the useless anxiety of one, and the incessant importunity of another; he began to repent of having devoted himself to a study, which was so narrow in its comprehension that it could never carry his name to any other country, and thought it unworthy of a man of parts to sell his life only for money. The barrenness of his fellow students forced him generally into other company at his hours of entertainment, and among the varieties of conversation through which his curiosity was daily wan-
10 dering, he, by chance, mingled at a tavern with some intelligent officers of the army. A man of letters was easily dazzled with the gaiety of their appearance, and softened into kindness by the politeness of their address; he, therefore, cultivated this new acquaintance, and when he saw how readily they found in every place admission and regard, and how familiarly they mingled with every rank and order of men, he began to feel his heart beat for military honours, and wondered how the prejudices of the university should make him so long insensible of that
20 ambition, which has fired so many hearts in every age, and negligent of that calling, which is, above all others, univer-sally and invariably illustrious, and which gives, even to the exterior appearance of its professors, a dignity and freedom unknown to the rest of mankind.

These favourable impressions were made still deeper by his conversation with ladies, whose regard for soldiers he could not observe, without wishing himself one of that happy fraternity, to which the female world seemed to have devoted their charms and their kindness. The love of
30 knowledge, which was still his predominant inclination, was gratified by the recital of adventures, and accounts of foreign countries; and, therefore, he concluded that there was no way of life, in which all his views could so compleatly concenter as in that of a soldier. In the art of war he thought it not difficult to excel, having observed

his new friends not very much versed in the principles of tacticks or fortification; he therefore studied all the military writers both antient and modern, and, in a short time, could tell how to have gained every remarkable battle that has been lost from the beginning of the world. He often shewed at table how Alexander should have been check'd in his conquests, what was the fatal error at Pharsalia, how Charles of Sweden might have escaped his ruin at Pultowa, and Marlborough might have been made to repent his temerity at Blenheim.   He entrenched armies 10 upon paper, so that no superiority of numbers could force them, and modelled in clay many impregnable fortresses, on which all the present arts of attack would be exhausted without effect.

Polyphilus, in a short time, obtained a commission; but before he could rub off the solemnity of a scholar, and gain the true air of military vivacity, a war was declared, and forces sent to the continent.   Here Polyphilus unhappily found that study alone would not make a soldier; for being much accustomed to think, he let the sense of 20 danger sink into his mind, and felt at the approach of any action that terror which a sentence of death would have brought upon him.   He saw that, instead of conquering their fears, the endeavour of his gay friends was only to escape them; but his philosophy chained his mind to its object, and rather loaded him with shackles than furnished him with arms.   He, however, suppressed his misery in silence, and passed through the campaign with honour, but found himself utterly unable to support another.

He then had recourse again to his books, and continued 30 to range from one study to another.   As I usually visit him once a month, and am admitted to him without previous notice, I have found him, within this last half year, decyphering the Chinese language, making a farce, collecting a vocabulary of the obsolete terms of the English law, writing an inquiry concerning the ancient Corinthian brass, and forming a new scheme of the variations of the needle.

Thus is this powerful genius, which might have extended the sphere of any science, or benefited the world in any profession, dissipated in a boundless variety, without profit to others or himself. He makes sudden irruptions into the regions of knowledge, and sees all obstacles give way before him ; but he never stays long enough to compleat his
10 conquest, to establish laws, or bring away the spoils.

Such is often the folly of men, whom nature has enabled to obtain skill and knowledge, on terms so easy, that they have no sense of the value of the acquisition ; they are qualified to make such speedy progress in learning, that they think themselves at liberty to loiter in the way, and by turning aside after every new object, lose the race, like Atalanta, to slower competitors, who press diligently forward, and whose force is directed to a single point.

I have often thought those happy that have been fixed,
20 from the first dawn of thought, in a determination to some state of life, by the choice of one, whose authority may preclude caprice, and whose influence may prejudice them in favour of his opinion. The general precept of consulting the genius is of little use, unless we are told, how the genius can be known. If it is to be discovered only by experiment, life will be lost, before the resolution can be fixed ; if any other indications are to be found, they may, perhaps, be very early discerned. At least, if to miscarry in an attempt be a proof of having mistaken the direction of the genius,
30 men appear not less frequently deceived with regard to themselves than to others ; and, therefore, no one has much reason to complain that his life was planned out by his friends, or to be confident that he should have had either more honour, or happiness, by being abandoned to the chance of his own fancy.

It was said of the learned bishop Sanderson, that, when he was preparing his lectures, he hesitated so much, and rejected so often, that, at the time of reading, he was often forced to produce, not what was best, but what happened to be at hand. This will be the state of every man, who, in the choice of his employment, balances all the arguments on every side ; the complication is so intricate, the motives and objections so numerous, there is so much play for the imagination, and so much remains in the power of others, that reason is forced at last to rest in neutrality, the decision devolves into the hands of chance, and after a great part of life spent in inquiries which can never be resolved, the rest must often pass in repenting the unnecessary delay, and can be useful to few other purposes than to warn others against the same folly, and to show, that of two states of life, equally consistent with religion and virtue, he who chuses earliest chuses best.

From *THE PLAN of a DICTIONARY*
OF THE ENGLISH LANGUAGE

Addressed to the Right Honourable Philip Dormer,
Earl of Chesterfield.

Published 1747.

WHEN I survey the Plan which I have laid before you, I cannot, my Lord, but confess, that I am frighted at its extent, and, like the soldiers of *Cæsar*, look on *Britain* as a new world, which it is almost madness to invade. But I hope, that though I should not complete the conquest, I shall at least discover the coast, civilize part of the inhabitants, and make it easy for some other adventurer to proceed farther, to reduce them wholly to subjection, and settle them under laws.

10 We are taught by the great *Roman* orator, that every man should propose to himself the highest degree of excellence, but that he may stop with honour at the second or third : though therefore my performance should fall below the excellence of other dictionaries, I may obtain, at least, the praise of having endeavoured well ; nor shall I think it any reproach to my diligence, that I have retired without a triumph, from a contest with united academies, and long successions of learned compilers. I cannot hope, in the warmest moments, to preserve so much caution through so 20 long a work, as not often to sink into negligence, or to obtain so much knowledge of all its parts as not frequently to fail by ignorance. I expect that sometimes the desire of accuracy will urge me to superfluities, and sometimes the fear of prolixity betray me to omissions : that in the extent of such variety, I shall be often bewildered ; and in the mazes of such intricacy, be frequently entangled ; that in

one part refinement will be subtilised beyond exactness, and evidence dilated in another beyond perspicuity. Yet I do not despair of approbation from those who, knowing the uncertainty of conjecture, the scantiness of knowledge, the fallibility of memory, and the unsteadiness of attention, can compare the causes of error with the means of avoiding it, and the extent of art with the capacity of man.

From the PREFACE to
A DICTIONARY OF THE ENGLISH LANGUAGE

Published 1755.

WHEN I first collected these authorities, I was desirous that every quotation should be useful to some other end than the illustration of a word ; I therefore extracted from philosophers principles of science ; from historians remarkable facts ; from chymists complete processes ; from divines striking exhortations ; and from poets beautiful descriptions. Such is design, while it is yet at a distance from execution. When the time called upon me to range this accumulation of elegance and wisdom into an alphabetical series, I soon discovered that the bulk of my volumes would fright away the student, and was forced to depart from my scheme of including all that was pleasing or useful in *English* literature, and reduce my transcripts very often to clusters of words, in which scarcely any meaning is retained ; thus to the weariness of copying, I was condemned to add the vexation of expunging. Some passages I have yet spared, which may relieve the labour of verbal searches, and intersperse with verdure and flowers the dusty desarts of barren philology.

The examples, thus mutilated, are no longer to be considered as conveying the sentiments or doctrine of their authours; the word for the sake of which they are inserted, with all its appendant clauses, has been carefully preserved; but it may sometimes happen, by hasty detruncation, that the general tendency of the sentence may be changed: the divine may desert his tenets, or the philosopher his system.

Some of the examples have been taken from writers who were never mentioned as masters of elegance or models of style; but words must be sought where they are used; and in what pages, eminent for purity, can terms of manufacture or agriculture be found? Many quotations serve no other purpose, than that of proving the bare existence of words, and are therefore selected with less scrupulousness than those which are to teach their structures and relations.

My purpose was to admit no testimony of living authours, that I might not be misled by partiality, and that none of my contemporaries might have reason to complain; nor have I departed from this resolution, but when some performance of uncommon excellence excited my veneration, when my memory supplied me, from late books, with an example that was wanting, or when my heart, in the tenderness of friendship, solicited admission for a favourite name.

So far have I been from any care to grace my pages with modern decorations, that I have studiously endeavoured to collect examples and authorities from the writers before the restoration, whose works I regard as *the wells of English undefiled*, as the pure sources of genuine diction. Our language, for almost a century, has, by the concurrence of many causes, been gradually departing from its original *Teutonick* character, and deviating towards a *Gallick* structure and phraseology, from which it ought to be our endeavour to recal it, by making our ancient volumes the ground-work of style, admitting among the additions of later times, only such as may supply real deficiencies, such as are readily adopted by the genius of our tongue, and incorporate easily with our native idioms.

But as every language has a time of rudeness antecedent to perfection, as well as of false refinement and declension, I have been cautious lest my zeal for antiquity might drive me into times too remote, and crowd my book with words now no longer understood. I have fixed *Sidney's* work for the boundary, beyond which I make few excursions. From the authours which rose in the time of *Elizabeth,* a speech 10 might be formed adequate to all the purposes of use and elegance. If the language of theology were extracted from *Hooker* and the translation of the Bible; the terms of natural knowledge from *Bacon* ; the phrases of policy, war, and navigation from *Raleigh* ; the dialect of poetry and fiction from *Spenser* and *Sidney* ; and the diction of common life from *Shakespeare,* few ideas would be lost to mankind, for want of *English* words, in which they might be expressed.

* * * * * * * * *

To have attempted much is always laudable, even when the enterprize is above the strength that undertakes it : To 20 rest below his own aim is incident to every one whose fancy is active, and whose views are comprehensive ; nor is any man satisfied with himself because he has done much, but because he can conceive little. When first I engaged in this work, I resolved to leave neither words nor things unexamined, and pleased myself with a prospect of the hours which I should revel away in feasts of literature, the obscure recesses of northern learning which I should enter and ransack, the treasures with which I expected every search into those neglected mines to reward my labour, and the 30 triumph with which I should display my acquisitions to mankind. When I had thus enquired into the original of words, I resolved to show likewise my attention to things ; to pierce deep into every science, to enquire the nature of every substance of which I inserted the name, to limit every idea by a definition strictly logical, and exhibit every production of art or nature in an accurate description, that my book might be in place of all other dictionaries whether appellative or technical. But these were the dreams of a poet doomed at last to wake a lexicographer.

*   *   *   *   *   *   *   *   *

If the changes that we fear be thus irresistible, what remains but to acquiesce with silence, as in the other insurmountable distresses of humanity ? It remains that we
10 retard what we cannot repel, that we palliate what we cannot cure. Life may be lengthened by care, though death cannot be ultimately defeated : tongues, like governments, have a natural tendency to degeneration; we have long preserved our constitution, let us make some struggles for our language.

In hope of giving longevity to that which its own nature forbids to be immortal, I have devoted this book, the labour of years, to the honour of my country, that we may no longer yield the palm of philology, without a contest, to
20 the nations of the continent. The chief glory of every people arises from its authours : whether I shall add any thing by my own writings to the reputation of *English* literature, must be left to time : much of my life has been lost under the pressures of disease ; much has been trifled away ; and much has always been spent in provision for the day that was passing over me ; but I shall not think my employment useless or ignoble, if by my assistance foreign nations, and distant ages, gain access to the propagators of knowledge, and understand the teachers of truth ; if my
30 labours afford light to the repositories of science, and add celebrity to *Bacon*, to *Hooker*, to *Milton*, and to *Boyle*.

When I am animated by this wish, I look with pleasure on my book, however defective, and deliver it to the world with the spirit of a man that has endeavoured well. That it will

immediately become popular I have not promised to myself :
a few wild blunders, and risible absurdities, from which no
work of such multiplicity was ever free, may for a time
furnish folly with laughter, and harden ignorance in contempt ; but useful diligence will at last prevail, and there
never can be wanting some who distinguish desert ; who will
consider that no dictionary of a living tongue ever can be
perfect, since, while it is hastening to publication, some
words are budding, and some falling away ; that a whole life
cannot be spent upon syntax and etymology, and that even 10
a whole life would not be sufficient ; that he, whose design
includes whatever language can express, must often speak
of what he does not understand; that a writer will sometimes be hurried by eagerness to the end, and sometimes
faint with weariness under a task, which *Scaliger* compares
to the labours of the anvil and the mine ; that what is
obvious is not always known, and what is known is not
always present ; that sudden fits of inadvertency will surprise vigilance, slight avocations will seduce attention, and
casual eclipses of the mind will darken learning ; and that 20
the writer shall often in vain trace his memory at the
moment of need, for that which yesterday he knew with
intuitive readiness, and which will come uncalled into his
thoughts to-morrow.

In this work, when it shall be found that much is omitted,
let it not be forgotten that much likewise is performed ;
and though no book was ever spared out of tenderness to the
authour, and the world is little solicitous to know whence
proceeded the faults of that which it condemns ; yet it may
gratify curiosity to inform it, that the *English Dictionary* 30
was written with little assistance of the learned, and without
any patronage of the great ; not in the soft obscurities of
retirement, or under the shelter of academick bowers, but
amidst inconvenience and distraction, in sickness and in
sorrow. It may repress the triumph of malignant criticism

to observe, that if our language is not here fully displayed, I
have only failed in an attempt which no human powers have
hitherto completed. If the lexicons of ancient tongues, now
immutably fixed, and comprized in a few volumes, be yet,
after the toil of successive ages, inadequate and delusive ; if
the aggregated knowledge, and co-operating diligence of the
Italian academicians, did not secure them from the censure
of *Beni* ; if the embodied criticks of *France*, when fifty years
had been spent upon their work, were obliged to change its
10 œconomy, and give their second edition another form, I may
surely be contented without the praise of perfection, which,
if I could obtain, in this gloom of solitude, what would it
avail me ? I have protracted my work till most of those
whom I wished to please have sunk into the grave, and
success and miscarriage are empty sounds : I therefore
dismiss it with frigid tranquillity, having little to fear or
hope from censure or from praise.

SPECIMEN ARTICLES

TORY. *n.s.* [A cant term, derived, I suppose, from an Irish
word signifying a savage.] One who adheres to the
ancient constitution of the state, and the apostolical
hierarchy of the church of England ; opposed to a *whig*.

The knight is more a *tory* in the country than the town, because
it more advances his interest.   *Addison*.

This Protestant zealot, this English divine,
In church and in state was of principles sound ;
Was truer than steel to the Hanover line,
And griev'd that a *tory* should live above ground.
                                                        Swift.

To confound his hated coin,
All parties and religions join,
Whigs, *tories*.   *Swift*.

WHIG. *n.s.* [Saxon.] 1. Whey. 2. The name of a faction.

(2) . . . from Scotland the word was brought into England, where
it is now one of our unhappy terms of disunion.   *Burnet*.
Whoever has a true value for church and state, should avoid the
extremes of *whig* for the sake of the former, and the extremes of
tory on the account of the latter.   *Swift*.

From *THE IDLER*

Published in the Universal Chronicle, *every Saturday from April 15, 1758, to April 5, 1760.*

NUMBER 10.   SATURDAY, *June* 17, 1758.

CREDULITY, or confidence of opinion too great for the evidence from which opinion is derived, we find to be a general weakness imputed by every sect and party to all others, and indeed by every man to every other man.

Of all kinds of credulity, the most obstinate and wonderful is that of political zealots ; of men, who being numbered, they know not how or why, in any of the parties that divide a state, resign the use of their own eyes and ears, and resolve to believe nothing that does not favour those whom they profess to follow.

The bigot of philosophy is seduced by authorities which he has not always opportunities to examine, is intangled in systems by which truth and falsehood are inextricably complicated, or undertakes to talk on subjects which nature did not form him able to comprehend.

The Cartesian, who denies that his horse feels the spur, or that the hare is afraid when the hounds approach her ; the disciple of *Malbranche*, who maintains that the man was not hurt by the bullet, which, according to vulgar apprehension, swept away his legs ; the follower of *Berkeley*, who, while he sits writing at his table, declares that he has neither table, paper, nor fingers ; have all the honour at least of being deceived by fallacies not easily detected, and may plead that they did not forsake truth, but for appearances which they were not able to distinguish from it.

But the man who engages in a party has seldom to do with any thing remote or abstruse. The present state of things is before his eyes; and, if he cannot be satisfied without retrospection, yet he seldom extends his views beyond the historical events of the last century. All the knowledge that he can want is within his attainment, and most of the arguments which he can hear are within his capacity.

Yet so it is that an *Idler* meets every hour of his life with
10 men who have different opinions upon every thing past, present, and future; who deny the most notorious facts, contradict the most cogent truths, and persist in asserting to-day what they asserted yesterday, in defiance of evidence, and contempt of confutation.

Two of my companions, who are grown old in idleness, are *Tom Tempest* and *Jack Sneaker*. Both of them consider themselves as neglected by their parties, and therefore intitled to credit, for why should they favour ingratitude? They are both men of integrity, where no factious interest
20 is to be promoted, and both lovers of truth, when they are not heated with political debate.

Tom Tempest is a steady friend to the house of *Stuart*. He can recount the prodigies that have appeared in the sky, and the calamities that have afflicted the nation every year from the revolution, and is of opinion, that if the exiled family had continued to reign, there would have neither been worms in our ships nor caterpillars on our trees. He wonders that the nation was not awakened by the hard frost to a revocation of the true king, and is hourly afraid
30 that the whole island will be lost in the sea. He believes that king *William* burned *Whitehall* that he might steal the furniture, and that *Tillotson* died an atheist. Of queen *Anne* he speaks with more tenderness, owns that she meant well, and can tell by whom and why she was poisoned. In the succeeding reigns all has been corruption, malice, and

design. He believes that nothing ill has ever happened
for these forty years by chance or error ; he holds that the
battle of *Dettingen* was won by mistake, and that of *Fontenoy*
lost by contract ; that the *Victory* was sunk by a private
order ; that *Cornhill* was fired by emissaries from the
council ; and the arch of *Westminster-bridge* was so contrived as to sink on purpose that the nation might be put
to charge. He considers the new road to *Islington* as an
encroachment on liberty, and often asserts that *broad wheels*
will be the ruin of *England*.   10

Tom is generally vehement and noisy, but nevertheless
has some secrets which he always communicates in a
whisper. Many and many a time has *Tom* told me, in
a corner, that our miseries were almost at an end, and that
we should see, in a month, another monarch on the throne ;
the time elapses without a revolution ; *Tom* meets me
again with new intelligence, the whole scheme is now settled,
and we shall see great events in another month.

Jack Sneaker is a hearty adherent to the present establishment ; he has known those who saw the bed into which   20
the pretender was conveyed in a warming-pan. He often
rejoices that the nation was not enslaved by the *Irish*. He
believes that king *William* never lost a battle, and that if
he had lived one year longer he would have conquered
France. He holds that *Charles* the first was a papist. He
allows there were some good men in the reign of queen
Anne, but the peace of *Utrecht* brought a blast upon the
nation, and has been the cause of all the evil that we have
suffered to the present hour. He believes that the scheme
of the *South Sea* was well intended, but that it miscarried 30
by the influence of *France*. He considers a standing army
as the bulwark of liberty, thinks us secured from corruption
by septennial parliaments, relates how we are enriched and
strengthened by the electoral dominions, and declares that
the publick debt is a blessing to the nation.

Yet amidst all this prosperity, poor *Jack* is hourly
disturbed by the dread of popery. He wonders that some
stricter laws are not made against papists, and is sometimes
afraid that they are busy with *French* gold among the
bishops and judges.

He cannot believe that the nonjurors are so quiet for
nothing, they must certainly be forming some plot for the
establishment of popery; he does not think the present
oaths sufficiently binding, and wishes that some better
10 security could be found for the succession of *Hanover*. He
is zealous for the naturalization of foreign protestants, and
rejoiced at the admission of the *Jews* to the *English* privileges, because he thought a *Jew* would never be a papist.

NUMBER 60.   SATURDAY, *June* 9, 1759.

Criticism is a study by which men grow important and
formidable at very small expence. The power of invention
has been conferred by nature upon few, and the labour of
learning those sciences which may by mere labour be
obtained is too great to be willingly endured; but every
man can exert such judgment as he has upon the works
20 of others; and he whom nature has made weak, and
idleness keeps ignorant, may yet support his vanity by the
name of a critick.

I hope it will give comfort to great numbers who are
passing through the world in obscurity, when I inform them
how easily distinction may be obtained. All the other
powers of literature are coy and haughty, they must be
long courted, and at last are not always gained; but
criticism is a goddess easy of access and forward of advance,
who will meet the slow, and encourage the timorous; the
30 want of meaning she supplies with words, and the want of
spirit she recompenses with malignity.

This profession has one recommendation peculiar to

itself, that it gives vent to malignity without real mischief. No genius was ever blasted by the breath of criticks. The poison which, if confined, would have burst the heart, fumes away in empty hisses, and malice is set at ease with very little danger to merit. The critick is the only man whose triumph is without another's pain, and whose greatness does not rise upon another's ruin.

To a study at once so easy and so reputable, so malicious and so harmless, it cannot be necessary to invite my readers by a long or laboured exhortation ; it is sufficient, since all would be criticks if they could, to shew by one eminent example that all can be criticks if they will.

Dick Minim, after the common course of puerile studies, in which he was no great proficient, was put apprentice to a brewer, with whom he had lived two years, when his uncle died in the city, and left him a large fortune in the stocks. *Dick* had for six months before used the company of the lower players, of whom he had learned to scorn a trade, and being now at liberty to follow his genius, he resolved to be a man of wit and humour. That he might be properly initiated in his new character, he frequented the coffeehouses near the theatres, where he listened very diligently, day after day, to those who talked of language and sentiments, and unities and catastrophes, till by slow degrees he began to think that he understood something of the stage, and hoped in time to talk himself.

But he did not trust so much to natural sagacity, as wholly to neglect the help of books. When the theatres were shut, he retired to *Richmond* with a few select writers, whose opinions he impressed upon his memory by unwearied diligence ; and, when he returned with other wits to the town, was able to tell, in very proper phrases, that the chief business of art is to copy nature ; that a perfect writer is not to be expected, because genius decays as judgment increases ; that the great art is the art of blotting ; and that, according to the rule of *Horace*, every piece should be kept nine years.

Of the great authors he now began to display the characters, laying down as an universal position, that all had beauties and defects. His opinion was, that *Shakespear*, committing himself wholly to the impulse of nature, wanted that correctness which learning would have given him; and that *Jonson*, trusting to learning, did not sufficiently cast his eye on nature. He blamed the *stanza* of *Spenser*, and could not bear the *hexameters* of *Sidney*. *Denham* and *Waller* he held the first reformers of *English* numbers; and thought that if *Waller* could have obtained the strength of *Denham*, or *Denham* the sweetness of *Waller*, there had been nothing wanting to complete a poet. He often expressed his commiseration of *Dryden's* poverty, and his indignation at the age which suffered him to write for bread; he repeated with rapture the first lines of *All for Love*, but wondered at the corruption of taste which could bear anything so unnatural as rhyming tragedies. In *Otway* he found uncommon powers of moving the passions, but was disgusted by his general negligence, and blamed him for making a conspirator his hero; and never concluded his disquisition, without remarking how happily the sound of the clock is made to alarm the audience. *Southern* would have been his favourite, but that he mixes comick with tragick scenes, intercepts the natural course of the passions, and fills the mind with a wild confusion of mirth and melancholy. The versification of *Rowe* he thought too melodious for the stage, and too little varied in different passions. He made it the great fault of *Congreve*, that all his persons were wits, and that he always wrote with more art than nature. He considered *Cato* rather as a poem than a play, and allowed *Addison* to be the complete master of allegory and grave humour, but paid no great deference to him as a critick. He thought the chief merit of *Prior* was in his

easy tales and lighter poems, though he allowed that his
Solomon had many noble sentiments elegantly expressed.
In *Swift* he discovered an inimitable vein of irony, and an
easiness which all would hope and few would attain. *Pope*
he was inclined to degrade from a poet to a versifier, and
thought his numbers rather luscious than sweet. He often
lamented the neglect of *Phædra and Hippolitus*, and wished
to see the stage under better regulations.

These assertions passed commonly uncontradicted ; and
if now and then an opponent started up, he was quickly 10
repressed by the suffrages of the company, and *Minim* went
away from every dispute with elation of heart and increase
of confidence.

He now grew conscious of his abilities, and began to talk
of the present state of dramatick poetry ; wondered what
was become of the comick genius which supplied our
ancestors with wit and pleasantry, and why no writer
could be found that durst now venture beyond a farce.
He saw no reason for thinking that the vein of humour was
exhausted, since we live in a country where liberty suffers 20
every character to spread itself to its utmost bulk, and
which therefore produces more originals than all the rest
of the world together. Of tragedy he concluded business
to be the soul, and yet often hinted that love predominates
too much upon the modern stage.

He was now an acknowledged critick, and had his own
seat in a coffee-house, and headed a party in the pit.
Minim has more vanity than ill-nature, and seldom desires
to do much mischief ; he will perhaps murmur a little in the
ear of him that sits next him, but endeavours to influence 30
the audience to favour, by clapping when an actor exclaims
ye gods, or laments the misery of his country.

By degrees he was admitted to rehearsals, and many of
his friends are of opinion, that our present poets are
indebted to him for their happiest thoughts ; by his

contrivance the bell was rung twice in *Barbarossa*, and by
his persuasion the author of *Cleone* concluded his play
without a couplet ; for what can be more absurd, said
Minim, than that part of a play should be rhymed, and
part written in blank verse ? and by what acquisition of
faculties is the speaker, who never could find rhymes before,
enabled to rhyme at the conclusion of an act ?

He is the great investigator of hidden beauties, and is
particularly delighted when he finds *the sound an echo to the*
sense. He has read all our poets with particular attention
to this delicacy of versification, and wonders at the supine-
ness with which their works have been hitherto perused, so
that no man has found the sound of a drum in this distich,

> ' When pulpit, drum ecclesiastic,
> ' Was beat with fist instead of a stick ; '

and that the wonderful lines upon honour and a bubble
have hitherto passed without notice.

> ' Honour is like the glassy bubble,
> ' Which costs philosophers such trouble ;
> ' Where one part crack'd, the whole does fly,
> ' And wits are crack'd to find out why.'

In these verses, says *Minim*, we have two striking accommodations of the sound to the sense. It is impossible to
utter the two lines emphatically without an act like that
which they describe ; *bubble* and *trouble* causing a momen-
tary inflation of the cheeks by the retention of the breath,
which is afterwards forcibly emitted, as in the practice of
blowing bubbles. But the greatest excellence is in the third
line, which is *crack'd* in the middle to express a crack, and
then shivers into monosyllables. Yet has this diamond lain
neglected with common stones, and among the innumerable
admirers of *Hudibras* the observation of this superlative
passage has been reserved for the sagacity of *Minim*.

From *THE PRINCE OF ABISSINIA,*
A TALE

First published 1759 ; printed from the Fourth Edition, 1766.

CHAPTER VI

A DISSERTATION ON THE ART OF FLYING

AMONG the artists that had been allured into the happy valley, to labour for the accommodation and pleasure of its inhabitants, was a man eminent for his knowledge of the mechanick powers, who had contrived many engines both of use and recreation. By a wheel, which the stream turned, he forced the water into a tower, whence it was distributed to all the apartments of the palace. He erected a pavillion in the garden, around which he kept the air always cool by artificial showers. One of the groves, appropriated to the ladies, was ventilated by fans to which the rivulet that run 10 through it gave a constant motion ; and instruments of soft musick were placed at proper distances, of which some played by the impulse of the wind, and some by the power of the stream.

This artist was sometimes visited by Rasselas, who was pleased with every kind of knowledge, imagining that the time would come when all his acquisitions should be of use to him in the open world. He came one day to amuse himself in his usual manner, and found the master busy in building a sailing chariot: he saw that the design was practicable 20 upon a level surface, and with expressions of great esteem solicited its completion. The workman was pleased to find himself so much regarded by the prince. and resolved to

gain yet higher honours. ' Sir, said he, you have seen but
a small part of what the mechanick sciences can perform.
I have been long of opinion, that, instead of the tardy con-
veyance of ships and chariots, man might use the swifter
migration of wings ; that the fields of air are open to knowledge, and that only ignorance and idleness need crawl upon
the ground.'

This hint rekindled the prince's desire of passing the
mountains ; having seen what the mechanist had already
10 performed, he was willing to fancy that he could do more ;
yet resolved to enquire further before he suffered hope to
afflict him by disappointment. ' I am afraid, said he to the
artist, that your imagination prevails over your skill, and
that you now tell me rather what you wish than what you
know. Every animal has his element assigned him ; the
birds have the air, and man and beasts the earth.' ' So,
replied the mechanist, fishes have the water, in which yet
beasts can swim by nature, and men by art. He that can
swim needs not despair to fly : to swim is to fly in a grosser
20 fluid, and to fly is to swim in a subtler. We are only to proportion our power of resistance to the different density of
matter through which we are to pass. You will be necessarily upborn by the air, if you can renew any impulse
upon it, faster than the air can recede from the pressure.'

' But the exercise of swimming, said the prince, is very
laborious ; the strongest limbs are soon wearied ; I am
afraid the act of flying will be yet more violent, and wings
will be of no great use, unless we can fly further than we
can swim.'

30 ' The labour of rising from the ground, said the artist,
will be great, as we see it in the heavier domestick fowls ;
but, as we mount higher, the earth's attraction, and the
body's gravity, will be gradually diminished, till we shall
arrive at a region where the man will float in the air without
any tendency to fall : no care will then be necessary, but

to move forwards, which the gentlest impulse will effect. You, Sir, whose curiosity is so extensive, will easily conceive with what pleasure a philosopher, furnished with wings, and hovering in the sky, would see the earth, and all its inhabitants, rolling beneath him, and presenting to him successively, by its diurnal motion, all the countries within the same parallel. How must it amuse the pendent spectator to see the moving scene of land and ocean, cities and desarts! To survey with equal security the marts of trade, and the fields of battle; mountains infested by barbarians, 10 and fruitful regions gladdened by plenty, and lulled by peace! How easily shall we then trace the Nile through all his passage; pass over to distant regions, and examine the face of nature from one extremity of the earth to the other!'

'All this, said the prince, is much to be desired, but I am afraid that no man will be able to breathe in these regions of speculation and tranquillity. I have been told, that respiration is difficult upon lofty mountains, yet from these precipices, though so high as to produce great tenuity of air, it is very easy to fall: therefore I suspect, that from any 20 height, where life can be supported, there may be danger of too quick descent.'

'Nothing, replied the artist, will ever be attempted, if all possible objections must be first overcome. If you will favour my project, I will try the first flight at my own hazard. I have considered the structure of all volant animals, and find the folding continuity of the bat's wings most easily accommodated to the human form. Upon this model I shall begin my task to-morrow, and in a year expect to tower into the air beyond the malice and pursuit of man. 30 But I will work only on this condition, that the art shall not be divulged, and that you shall not require me to make wings for any but ourselves.'

'Why, said Rasselas, should you envy others so great an advantage? All skill ought to be exerted for universal good;

every man has owed much to others, and ought to repay the kindness that he has received.'

'If men were all virtuous, returned the artist, I should with great alacrity teach them all to fly. But what would be the security of the good, if the bad could at pleasure invade them from the sky? Against an army sailing through the clouds neither walls, nor mountains, nor seas, could afford any security. A flight of northern savages might hover in the wind, and light at once with irresistible violence upon
10 the capital of a fruitful region that was rolling under them. Even this valley, the retreat of princes, the abode of happiness, might be violated by the sudden descent of some of the naked nations that swarm on the coast of the southern sea.'

The prince promised secrecy, and waited for the performance, not wholly hopeless of success. He visited the work from time to time, observed its progress, and remarked many ingenious contrivances to facilitate motion, and unite levity with strength. The artist was every day more certain that he should leave vultures and eagles behind him, and
20 the contagion of his confidence seized upon the prince.

In a year the wings were finished, and, on a morning appointed, the maker appeared furnished for flight on a little promontory: he waved his pinions a while to gather air, then leaped from his stand, and in an instant dropped into the lake. His wings, which were of no use in the air, sustained him in the water, and the prince drew him to land, half dead with terror and vexation.

CHAPTER XXII

THE HAPPINESS OF A LIFE LED ACCORDING TO NATURE

Rasselas went often to an assembly of learned men, who met at stated times to unbend their minds, and compare
30 their opinions. Their manners were somewhat coarse, but their conversation was instructive, and their disputations

acute, though sometimes too violent, and often continued till
neither controvertist remembered upon what question they
began.   Some faults were almost general among them :
every one was desirous to dictate to the rest, and every one
was pleased to hear the genius or knowledge of another
depreciated.

In this assembly Rasselas was relating his interview with
the hermit, and the wonder with which he heard him censure
a course of life which he had so deliberately chosen, and so
laudably followed.   The sentiments of the hearers were 10
various.   Some were of opinion, that the folly of his choice
had been justly punished by condemnation to perpetual per-
severance.   One of the youngest among them, with great
vehemence, pronounced him an hypocrite.   Some talked of
the right of society to the labour of individuals, and considered retirement as a desertion of duty.   Others readily
allowed, that there was a time when the claims of the publick
were satisfied, and when a man might properly sequester
himself, to review his life, and purify his heart.

One, who appeared more affected with the narrative than 20
the rest, thought it likely, that the hermit would, in a few
years, go back to his retreat, and, perhaps, if shame did not
restrain, or death intercept him, return once more from his
retreat into the world : ' For the hope of happiness, said he,
is so strongly impressed, that the longest experience is not
able to efface it.   Of the present state, whatever it be, we
feel, and are forced to confess, the misery ; yet, when the
same state is again at a distance, imagination paints it as
desirable.   But the time will surely come, when desire will be
no longer our torment, and no man shall be wretched but by 30
his own fault.'

' This, said a philosopher, who had heard him with tokens
of great impatience, is the present condition of a wise man.
The time is already come, when none are wretched but by
their own fault.   Nothing is more idle, than to enquire after

happiness, which nature has kindly placed within our reach. The way to be happy is to live according to nature, in obedience to that universal and unalterable law with which every heart is originally impressed; which is not written on it by precept, but engraven by destiny, not instilled by education, but infused at our nativity. He that lives according to nature will suffer nothing from the delusions of hope, or importunities of desire : he will receive and reject with equability of temper ; and act or suffer as the
10 reason of things shall alternately prescribe. Other men may amuse themselves with subtle definitions, or intricate ratiocination. Let them learn to be wise by easier means : let them observe the hind of the forest, and the linnet of the grove : let them consider the life of animals, whose motions are regulated by instinct ; they obey their guide and are happy. Let us therefore, at length, cease to dispute, and learn to live ; throw away the incumbrance of precepts, which they who utter them with so much pride and pomp do not understand, and carry with us this simple and intelli-
20 gible maxim, That deviation from nature is deviation from happiness.'

When he had spoken, he looked round him with a placid air, and enjoyed the consciousness of his own beneficence. ' Sir, said the prince, with great modesty, as I, like all the rest of mankind, am desirous of felicity, my closest attention has been fixed upon your discourse : I doubt not the truth of a position which a man so learned has so confidently advanced. Let me only know what it is to live according to nature.'
30 ' When I find young men so humble and so docile, said the philosopher, I can deny them no information which my studies have enabled me to afford. To live according to nature, is to act always with due regard to the fitness arising from the relations and qualities of causes and effects ; to concur with the great and unchangeable scheme of uni-

versal felicity ; to co-operate with the general disposition
and tendency of the present system of things.'

The prince soon found that this was one of the sages whom
he should understand less as he heard him longer. He
therefore bowed and was silent, and the philosopher, supposing him satisfied, and the rest vanquished, rose up and
departed with the air of a man that had co-operated with
the present system.

CHAPTER XLV

THEY DISCOURSE WITH AN OLD MAN

The evening was now far past, and they rose to return
home. As they walked along the bank of the Nile, delighted
with the beams of the moon quivering on the water, they
saw at a small distance an old man, whom the prince had
often heard in the assembly of the sages. ' Yonder, said he,
is one whose years have calmed his passions, but not clouded
his reason : let us close the disquisitions of the night, by
enquiring what are his sentiments of his own state, that we
may know whether youth alone is to struggle with vexation,
and whether any better hope remains for the latter part of
life.'

Here the sage approached and saluted them. They
invited him to join their walk, and prattled a while as
acquaintance that had unexpectedly met one another. The
old man was chearful and talkative, and the way seemed
short in his company. He was pleased to find himself not
disregarded, accompanied them to their house, and, at the
prince's request, entered with them. They placed him in the
seat of honour, and set wine and conserves before him.

' Sir, said the princess, an evening walk must give to a
man of learning, like you, pleasures which ignorance and
youth can hardly conceive. You know the qualities and the

causes of all that you behold, the laws by which the river flows, the periods in which the planets perform their revolutions. Everything must supply you with contemplation, and renew the consciousness of your own dignity.'

' Lady, answered he, let the gay and the vigorous expect pleasure in their excursions, it is enough that age can obtain ease. To me the world has lost its novelty : I look round, and see what I remember to have seen in happier days. I rest against a tree, and consider, that in the same shade I 10 once disputed upon the annual overflow of the Nile with a friend who is now silent in the grave. I cast my eyes upwards, fix them on the changing moon, and think with pain on the vicissitudes of life. I have ceased to take much delight in physical truth ; for what have I to do with those things which I am soon to leave ? '

' You may at least recreate yourself, said Imlac, with the recollection of an honourable and useful life, and enjoy the praise which all agree to give you.'

' Praise, said the sage, with a sigh, is to an old man an 20 empty sound. I have neither mother to be delighted with the reputation of her son, nor wife to partake the honours of her husband. I have outlived my friends and my rivals. Nothing is now of much importance; for I cannot extend my interest beyond myself. Youth is delighted with applause, because it is considered as the earnest of some future good, and because the prospect of life is far extended : but to me, who am now declining to decrepitude, there is little to be feared from the malevolence of men, and yet less to be hoped from their affection or esteem. Something they may 30 yet take away, but they can give me nothing. Riches would now be useless, and high employment would be pain. My retrospect of life recalls to my view many opportunities of good neglected, much time squandered upon trifles, and more lost in idleness and vacancy. I leave many great designs unattempted, and many great attempts unfinished.

My mind is burthened with no heavy crime, and therefore
I compose myself to tranquility; endeavour to abstract my
thoughts from hopes and cares, which, though reason knows
them to be vain, still try to keep their old possession of
the heart; expect, with serene humility, that hour which
nature cannot long delay; and hope to possess in a better
state that happiness which here I could not find, and that
virtue which here I have not attained.'

He rose and went away, leaving his audience not much
elated with the hope of long life. The prince consoled him- 10
self with remarking, that it was not reasonable to be disappointed by this account; for age had never been considered as the season of felicity, and, if it was possible to be
easy in decline and weakness, it was likely that the days of
vigour and alacrity might be happy: that the noon of life
might be bright, if the evening could be calm.

The princess suspected that age was querulous and malignant, and delighted to repress the expectations of those who
had newly entered the world. She had seen the possessors
of estates look with envy on their heirs, and known many 20
who enjoy pleasure no longer than they can confine it to
themselves.

Pekuah conjectured, that the man was older than he
appeared, and was willing to impute his complaints to
delirious dejection; or else supposed that he had been
unfortunate, and was therefore discontented: 'For nothing,
said she, is more common than to call our own condition, the
condition of life.'

Imlac, who had no desire to see them depressed, smiled at
the comforts which they could so readily procure to them- 30
selves, and remembered, that at the same age, he was
equally confident of unmingled prosperity, and equally
fertile of consolatory expedients. He forbore to force upon
them unwelcome knowledge, which time itself would too
soon impress.

From JOHNSON'S EDITION OF SHAKESPEARE

Published 1765.

1 : From the PREFACE

THE Poet, of whose works I have undertaken the revision, may now begin to assume the dignity of an ancient, and claim the privilege of established fame and prescriptive veneration. He has long outlived his century, the term commonly fixed as the test of literary merit. Whatever advantages he might once derive from personal allusions, local customs, or temporary opinions, have for many years been lost ; and every topick of merriment, or motive of sorrow, which the modes of artificial life afforded
10 him, now only obscure the scenes which they once illuminated. The effects of favour and competition are at an end ; the tradition of his friendships and his enmities has perished ; his works support no opinion with arguments, nor supply any faction with invectives ; they can neither indulge vanity nor gratify malignity ; but are read without any other reason than the desire of pleasure, and are therefore praised only as pleasure is obtained ; yet, thus unassisted by interest or passion, they have past through variations of taste and changes of manners, and, as they
20 devolved from one generation to another, have received new honours at every transmission.

But because human judgment, though it be gradually gaining upon certainty, never becomes infallible ; and approbation, though long continued, may yet be only the approbation of prejudice or fashion ; it is proper to inquire,

by what peculiarities of excellence *Shakespeare* has gained
and kept the favour of his countrymen.

Nothing can please many, and please long, but just
representations of general nature. Particular manners can
be known to few, and therefore few only can judge how
nearly they are copied. The irregular combinations of
fanciful invention may delight a-while, by that novelty of
which the common satiety of life sends us all in quest ; but
the pleasures of sudden wonder are soon exhausted, and
the mind can only repose on the stability of truth.   10

Shakespeare is above all writers, at least above all modern
writers, the poet of nature ; the poet that holds up to his
readers a faithful mirrour of manners and of life. His
characters are not modified by the customs of particular
places, unpractised by the rest of the world ; by the
peculiarities of studies or professions, which can operate
but upon small numbers ; or by the accidents of transient
fashions or temporary opinions : they are the genuine
progeny of common humanity, such as the world will always
supply, and observation will always find. His persons act 20
and speak by the influence of those general passions and
principles by which all minds are agitated, and the whole
system of life is continued in motion. In the writings of
other poets a character is too often an individual ; in those
of *Shakespeare* it is commonly a species.

It is from this wide extension of design that so much
instruction is derived. It is this which fills the plays of
Shakespeare with practical axioms and domestick wisdom.
It was said of *Euripides*, that every verse was a precept ;
and it may be said of *Shakespeare*, that from his works may 30
be collected a system of civil and oeconomical prudence.
Yet his real power is not shewn in the splendour of particular
passages, but by the progress of his fable, and the tenour
of his dialogue ; and he that tries to recommend him by
select quotations, will succeed like the pedant in *Hierocles,*

who, when he offered his house to sale, carried a brick in his pocket as a specimen.

It will not easily be imagined how much *Shakespeare* excells in accommodating his sentiments to real life, but by comparing him with other authours. It was observed of the ancient schools of declamation, that the more diligently they were frequented, the more was the student disqualified for the world, because he found nothing there which he should ever meet in any other place. The same remark 10 may be applied to every stage but that of *Shakespeare*. The theatre, when it is under any other direction, is peopled by such characters as were never seen, conversing in a language which was never heard, upon topicks which will never arise in the commerce of mankind. But the dialogue of this authour is often so evidently determined by the incident which produces it, and is pursued with so much ease and simplicity, that it seems scarcely to claim the merit of fiction, but to have been gleaned by diligent selection out of common conversation, and common 20 occurrences.

Upon every other stage the universal agent is love, by whose power all good and evil is distributed, and every action quickened or retarded. To bring a lover, a lady and a rival into the fable ; to entangle them in contradictory obligations, perplex them with oppositions of interest, and harrass them with violence of desires inconsistent with each other ; to make them meet in rapture and part in agony ; to fill their mouths with hyperbolical joy and outrageous sorrow ; to distress them as nothing human ever was 30 distressed ; to deliver them as nothing human ever was delivered ; is the business of a modern dramatist. For this probability is violated, life is misrepresented, and language is depraved. But love is only one of many passions ; and as it has no great influence upon the sum of life, it has little operation in the dramas of a poet, who caught his ideas from the living world, and exhibited only what he saw before him. He knew, that any other passion, as it was regular or exorbitant, was a cause of happiness or calamity.

Characters thus ample and general were not easily discriminated and preserved, yet perhaps no poet ever kept his personages more distinct from each other. I will not say with *Pope*, that every speech may be assigned to the proper speaker, because many speeches there are which have nothing characteristical ; but perhaps, though some may be equally adapted to every person, it will be difficult 10 to find any, that can be properly transferred from the present possessor to another claimant. The choice is right, when there is reason for choice.

Other dramatists can only gain attention by hyperbolical or aggravated characters, by fabulous and unexampled excellence or depravity, as the writers of barbarous romances invigorated the reader by a giant and a dwarf ; and he that should form his expectations of human affairs from the play, or from the tale, would be equally deceived. *Shakespeare* has no heroes ; his scenes are occupied only by men, 20 who act and speak as the reader thinks that he should himself have spoken or acted on the same occasion : Even where the agency is supernatural the dialogue is level with life. Other writers disguise the most natural passions and most frequent incidents ; so that he who contemplates them in the book will not know them in the world : *Shakespeare* approximates the remote, and familiarizes the wonderful ; the event which he represents will not happen, but if it were possible, its effects would probably be such as he has assigned ; and it may be said, that he has not only 30 shewn human nature as it acts in real exigencies, but as it would be found in trials, to which it cannot be exposed.

This therefore is the praise of *Shakespeare*, that his drama is the mirrour of life ; that he who has mazed his imagination, in following the phantoms which other writers raise up before him, may here be cured of his delirious extasies, by reading human sentiments in human language; by scenes from which a hermit may estimate the transactions of the world, and a confessor predict the progress of the passions.

*   *   *   *   *   *   *

The force of his comick scenes has suffered little diminution from the changes made by a century and a half, in manners or in words. As his personages act upon principles arising from genuine passion, very little modified by particular forms, their pleasures and vexations are communicable to
10 all times and to all places; they are natural, and therefore durable; the adventitious peculiarities of personal habits, are only superficial dies, bright and pleasing for a little while, yet soon fading to a dim tinct, without any remains of former lustre; but the discriminations of true passion are the colours of nature; they pervade the whole mass, and can only perish with the body that exhibits them. The accidental compositions of heterogeneous modes are dissolved by the chance which combined them; but the uniform simplicity of primitive qualities neither admits
20 increase, nor suffers decay. The sand heaped by one flood is scattered by another, but the rock always continues in its place. The stream of time, which is continually washing the dissoluble fabricks of other poets, passes without injury by the adamant of *Shakespeare*.

If there be, what I believe there is, in every nation, a stile which never becomes obsolete, a certain mode of phraseology so consonant and congenial to the analogy and principles of its respective language as to remain settled and unaltered; this stile is probably to be sought in the
30 common intercourse of life, among those who speak only to be understood, without ambition of elegance. The polite are always catching modish innovations, and the learned depart from established forms of speech, in hope of finding or making better; those who wish for distinction forsake

the vulgar, when the vulgar is right; but there is a conversation above grossness and below refinement, where propriety resides, and where this poet seems to have gathered his comick dialogue. He is therefore more agreeable to the ears of the present age than any other authour equally remote, and among his other excellencies deserves to be studied as one of the original masters of our language.

* * * * * * *

Voltaire expresses his wonder, that our authour's extravagances are endured by a nation, which has seen the tragedy of *Cato*. Let him be answered, that *Addison* speaks the language of poets, and *Shakespeare*, of men. We find in *Cato* innumerable beauties which enamour us of its authour, but we see nothing that acquaints us with human sentiments or human actions; we place it with the fairest and the noblest progeny which judgment propagates by conjunction with learning, but *Othello* is the vigorous and vivacious offspring of observation impregnated by genius. *Cato* affords a splendid exhibition of artificial and fictitious manners, and delivers just and noble sentiments, in diction easy, elevated and harmonious, but its hopes and fears communicate no vibration to the heart; the composition refers us only to the writer; we pronounce the name of *Cato*, but we think on *Addison*.

The work of a correct and regular writer is a garden accurately formed and diligently planted, varied with shades, and scented with flowers; the composition of *Shakespeare* is a forest, in which oaks extend their branches, and pines tower in the air, interspersed sometimes with weeds and brambles, and sometimes giving shelter to myrtles and to roses; filling the eye with awful pomp, and gratifying the mind with endless diversity. Other poets display cabinets of precious rarities, minutely finished, wrought into shape, and polished into brightness. *Shakespeare* opens a mine which contains gold and diamonds in unexhaustible plenty, though clouded by incrustations, debased by impurities, and mingled with a mass of meaner minerals.

2 : From the Notes on *HAMLET*

Polonius is a man bred in courts, exercised in business, stored with observation, confident of his knowledge, proud of his eloquence, and declining into dotage. His mode of oratory is truly represented as designed to ridicule the practice of those times, of prefaces that made no introduction, and of method that embarrassed rather than explained.
10 This part of his character is accidental, the rest is natural. Such a man is positive and confident, because he knows that his mind was once strong, and knows not that it is become weak. Such a man excels in general principles, but fails in the particular application. He is knowing in retrospect, and ignorant in foresight. While he depends upon his memory, and can draw from his repositories of knowledge, he utters weighty sentences, and gives useful counsel ; but as the mind in its enfeebled state cannot be kept long busy and intent, the old man is subject to sudden
20 dereliction of his faculties, he loses the order of his ideas, and entangles himself in his own thoughts, till he recovers the leading principle, and falls again into his former train. This idea of dotage encroaching upon wisdom, will solve all the phænomena of the character of *Polonius*.

3 : From the Notes on *HENRY IV*

None of *Shakespeare's* plays are more read than the first and second parts of *Henry* the fourth. Perhaps no authour has ever in two plays afforded so much delight. The great events are interesting, for the fate of kingdoms depends upon them ; the slighter occurrences are diverting, and,
30 except one or two, sufficiently probable ; the incidents are

multiplied with wonderful fertility of invention, and the characters diversified with the utmost nicety of discernment, and the profoundest skill in the nature of man.

The prince, who is the hero both of the comick and tragick part, is a young man of great abilities and violent passions, whose sentiments are right, though his actions are wrong ; whose virtues are obscured by negligence, and whose understanding is dissipated by levity. In his idle hours he is rather loose than wicked, and when the occasion forces out his latent qualities, he is great without effort, and brave 10 without tumult. The trifler is roused into a hero, and the hero again reposes in the trifler. This character is great, original, and just.

Piercy is a rugged soldier, cholerick, and quarrelsome, and has only the soldier's virtues, generosity and courage.

But *Falstaff*, unimitated, unimitable *Falstaff*, how shall I describe thee ? Thou compound of sense and vice ; of sense which may be admired but not esteemed, of vice which may be despised, but hardly detested. *Falstaff* is a character loaded with faults, and with those faults which naturally 20 produce contempt. He is a thief, and a glutton, a coward, and a boaster, always ready to cheat the weak, and prey upon the poor ; to terrify the timorous and insult the defenceless. At once obsequious and malignant, he satirises in their absence those whom he lives by flattering. He is familiar with the prince only as an agent of vice, but of this familiarity he is so proud as not only to be supercilious and haughty with common men, but to think his interest of importance to the duke of *Lancaster*. Yet the man thus corrupt, thus despicable, makes himself necessary to the 30 prince that despises him, by the most pleasing of all qualities, perpetual gaiety, by an unfailing power of exciting laughter, which is the more freely indulged, as his wit is not of the splendid or ambitious kind, but consists in easy escapes and sallies of levity, which make sport but raise no envy. It must be observed that he is stained with no enormous or sanguinary crimes, so that his licentiousness is not so offensive but that it may be borne for his mirth.

The moral to be drawn from this representation is, that no man is more dangerous than he that with a will to corrupt, hath the power to please ; and that neither wit nor honesty ought to think themselves safe with such a companion when they see *Henry* seduced by *Falstaff*.

4 : From the Notes on *MACBETH*

Act II. Scene v.   (ii. iii. 118–21.)

10   *Here, lay* Duncan ;
His silver skin laced with his golden blood,
And his gash'd stabs look'd like a breach in nature
For Ruin's wasteful entrance.

Mr. *Pope* has endeavoured to improve one of these lines by substituting *goary blood* for *golden blood* ; but it may easily be admitted that he who could on such an occasion talk of *lacing the silver skin*, would *lace it* with *golden blood*. No amendment can be made to this line, of which every word is equally faulty, but by a general blot.

20   It is not improbable, that *Shakespeare* put these forced and unnatural metaphors into the mouth of *Macbeth* as a mark of artifice and dissimulation, to show the difference between the studied language of hypocrisy, and the natural outcries of sudden passion. This whole speech so considered, is a remarkable instance of judgment, as it consists entirely of antithesis and metaphor.

From *Thoughts on the late Transactions Respecting FALKLAND'S ISLANDS*

Published 1771.

As war is the last of remedies, *cuncta prius tentanda,* all lawful expedients must be used to avoid it. As war is the extremity of evil, it is surely the duty of those whose station intrusts them with the care of nations, to avert it from their charge. There are diseases of animal nature which nothing but amputation can remove ; so there may, by the depravation of human passions, be sometimes a gangrene in collective life for which fire and the sword are the necessary remedies ; but in what can skill or caution be better shown than preventing such dreadful 10 operations, while there is yet room for gentler methods ?

It is wonderful with what coolness and indifference the greater part of mankind see war commenced. Those that hear of it at a distance, or read of it in books, but have never presented its evils to their minds, consider it as little more than a splendid game ; a proclamation, an army, a battle, and a triumph. Some indeed must perish in the most successful field, but they die upon the bed of honour, *resign their lives amidst the joys of conquest, and, filled with England's glory, smile in death.*   20

The life of a modern soldier is ill represented by heroick fiction. War has means of destruction more formidable than the cannon and the sword. Of the thousands and ten thousands that perished in our late contests with France and Spain, a very small part ever felt the stroke of an enemy ; the rest languished in tents and ships amidst damps and putrefaction ; pale, torpid, spiritless, and

helpless; gasping and groaning unpitied among men made
obdurate by long continuance of hopeless misery; and were
at last whelmed in pits, or heaved into the ocean, without
notice and without remembrance. By incommodious en-
campments and unwholesome stations, where courage is
useless, and enterprise impracticable, fleets are silently
dispeopled, and armies sluggishly melted away.

Thus is a people gradually exhausted, for the most part
with little effect. The wars of civilized nations make very
10 slow changes in the system of empire. The publick per-
ceives scarcely any alteration but an increase of debt;
and the few individuals who are benefited, are not supposed
to have the clearest right to their advantages. If he that
shared the danger enjoyed the profit; if he that bled
in the battle grew rich by the victory, he might shew his
gains without envy. But at the conclusion of a ten years
war, how are we recompensed for the death of multitudes
and the expence of millions, but by contemplating the
sudden glories of paymasters and agents, contractors and
20 commissaries, whose equipages shine like meteors and
whose palaces rise like exhalations.

These are the men who, without virtue, labour, or hazard,
are growing rich as their country is impoverished; they
rejoice when obstinacy or ambition adds another year to
slaughter and devastation; and laugh from their desks
at bravery and science, while they are adding figure to
figure, and cipher to cipher, hoping for a new contract from
a new armament, and computing the profits of a siege
or tempest.

30   Those who suffer their minds to dwell on these considera-
tions will think it no great crime in the ministry that they
have not snatched with eagerness the first opportunity of
rushing into the field, when they were able to obtain by
quiet negotiation all the real good that victory could have
brought us.

From *A JOURNEY to the*
WESTERN ISLANDS OF SCOTLAND

Published 1775.

It will very readily occur, that this uniformity of barrenness can afford very little amusement to the traveller ;
that it is easy to sit at home and conceive rocks and heath,
and waterfalls ; and that these journeys are useless labours,
which neither impregnate the imagination, nor enlarge the
understanding. It is true that of far the greater part of
things, we must content ourselves with such knowledge as
description may exhibit, or analogy supply ; but it is true
likewise, that these ideas are always incomplete, and that
at least, till we have compared them with realities, we do 10
not know them to be just. As we see more, we become
possessed of more certainties, and consequently gain more
principles of reasoning, and found a wider basis of analogy.

Regions mountainous and wild, thinly inhabited, and
little cultivated, make a great part of the earth, and he
that has never seen them, must live unacquainted with
much of the face of nature, and with one of the great
scenes of human existence.

As the day advanced towards noon, we entered a narrow
valley not very flowery, but sufficiently verdant. Our 20
guides told us, that the horses could not travel all day
without rest or meat, and intreated us to stop here, because
no grass would be found in any other place. The request
was reasonable and the argument cogent. We therefore
willingly dismounted and diverted ourselves as the place
gave us opportunity.

I sat down on a bank, such as a writer of Romance might have delighted to feign. I had indeed no trees to whisper over my head, but a clear rivulet streamed at my feet. The day was calm, the air soft, and all was rudeness, silence, and solitude. Before me, and on either side, were high hills, which by hindering the eye from ranging, forced the mind to find entertainment for itself. Whether I spent the hour well I know not; for here I first conceived the thought of this narration.

10 We were in this place at ease and by choice, and had no evils to suffer or to fear; yet the imaginations excited by the view of an unknown and untravelled wilderness are not such as arise in the artificial solitude of parks and gardens, a flattering notion of self-sufficiency, a placid indulgence of voluntary delusions, a secure expansion of the fancy, or a cool concentration of the mental powers. The phantoms which haunt a desert are want, and misery, and danger; the evils of dereliction rush upon the thoughts; man is made unwillingly acquainted with his own weakness, 20 and meditation shews him only how little he can sustain, and how little he can perform. There were no traces of inhabitants, except perhaps a rude pile of clods called a summer hut, in which a herdsman had rested in the favourable seasons. Whoever had been in the place where I then sat, unprovided with provisions and ignorant of the country, might, at least before the roads were made, have wandered among the rocks, till he had perished with hardship, before he could have found either food or shelter. Yet what are these hillocks to the ridges of Taurus, or 30 these spots of wildness to the desarts of America?

* * * * * * *

There seems now, whatever be the cause, to be through a great part of the Highlands a general discontent. That adherence, which was lately professed by every man to the chief of his name, has now little prevalence; and he that cannot live as he desires at home, listens to the tale of fortunate islands, and happy regions, where every man may have land of his own, and eat the product of his labour without a superior.

Those who have obtained grants of American lands, have, as is well known, invited settlers from all quarters of the globe ; and among other places, where oppression might produce a wish for new habitations, their emissaries would not fail to try their persuasions in the Isles of Scotland, where at the time when the clans were newly 10 disunited from their Chiefs, and exasperated by unprecedented exactions, it is no wonder that they prevailed.

Whether the mischiefs of emigration were immediately perceived, may be justly questioned. They who went first, were probably such as could best be spared ; but the accounts sent by the earliest adventurers, whether true or false, inclined many to follow them ; and whole neighbourhoods formed parties for removal ; so that departure from their native country is no longer exile. He that goes thus accompanied, carries with him all that makes life 20 pleasant. He sits down in a better climate, surrounded by his kindred and his friends : they carry with them their language, their opinions, their popular songs, and hereditary merriment : they change nothing but the place of their abode ; and of that change they perceive the benefit.

This is the real effect of emigration, if those that go away together settle on the same spot, and preserve their ancient union. But some relate that these adventurous visitants of unknown regions, after a voyage passed in dreams of plenty and felicity, are dispersed at last upon 30 a Sylvan wilderness, where their first years must be spent in toil, to clear the ground which is afterwards to be tilled, and that the whole effect of their undertaking is only more fatigue and equal scarcity.

Both accounts may be suspected. Those who are gone

will endeavour by every art to draw others after them ; for as their numbers are greater, they will provide better for themselves. When *Nova Scotia* was first peopled, I remember a letter, published under the character of a New Planter, who related how much the climate put him in mind of Italy. Such intelligence the *Hebridians* probably receive from their transmarine correspondents. But with equal temptations of interest, and perhaps with no greater niceness of veracity, the owners of the Islands 10 spread stories of American hardships to keep their people content at home.

Some method to stop this epidemick desire of wandering, which spreads its contagion from valley to valley, deserves to be sought with great diligence. In more fruitful countries, the removal of one only makes room for the succession of another : but in the *Hebrides*, the loss of an inhabitant leaves a lasting vacuity ; for nobody born in any other parts of the world will choose this country for his residence ; and an Island once depopulated will remain a desert, as 20 long as the present facility of travel gives every one, who is discontented and unsettled, the choice of his abode.

Let it be inquired, whether the first intention of those who are fluttering on the wing, and collecting a flock that they may take their flight, be to attain good, or to avoid evil. If they are dissatisfied with that part of the globe, which their birth has allotted them, and resolve not to live without the pleasures of happier climates ; if they long for bright suns, and calm skies, and flowery fields, and fragrant 30 gardens, I know not by what eloquence they can be persuaded, or by what offers they can be hired to stay.

But if they are driven from their native country by positive evils, and disgusted by ill-treatment, real or imaginary, it were fit to remove their grievances, and quiet their resentment ; since, if they have been hitherto undutiful subjects, they will not much mend their principles by American conversation.

To allure them into the army, it was thought proper to indulge them in the continuance of their national dress. If this concession could have any effect, it might easily be made. That dissimilitude of appearance, which was supposed to keep them distinct from the rest of the nation, might disincline them from coalescing with the *Pennsylvanians*, or people of *Connecticut*. If the restitution of their arms will reconcile them to their country, let them 10 have again those weapons, which will not be more mischievous at home than in the Colonies. That they may not fly from the increase of rent, I know not whether the general good does not require that the landlords be, for a time, restrained in their demands, and kept quiet by pensions proportionate to their loss.

To hinder insurrection, by driving away the people, and to govern peaceably, by having no subjects, is an expedient that argues no great profundity of politicks. To soften the obdurate, to convince the mistaken, to mollify the 20 resentful, are worthy of a statesman ; but it affords a legislator little self-applause to consider, that where there was formerly an insurrection, there is now a wilderness.

*   *   *   *   *   *   *

Not long after we came to another range of black rocks, which had the appearance of broken pilasters, set one behind another to a great depth. This place was chosen by Sir *Allan* for our dinner. We were easily accommodated with seats, for the stones were of all heights, and refreshed ourselves and our boatmen, who could have no other rest till we were at *Icolmkill*.   30

The evening was now approaching, and we were yet at a considerable distance from the end of our expedition. We could therefore stop no more to make remarks in the way, but set forward with some degree of eagerness. The

day soon failed us, and the moon presented a very solemn
and pleasing scene. The sky was clear, so that the eye
commanded a wide circle : the sea was neither still nor
turbulent : the wind neither silent nor loud. We were
never far from one coast or another, on which, if the weather
had become violent, we could have found shelter, and therefore contemplated at ease the region through which we
glided in the tranquillity of the night, and saw now a rock
and now an island grow gradually conspicuous and gradually
10 obscure. I committed the fault which I have just been
censuring, in neglecting, as we passed, to note the series of
this placid navigation.

We were very near an Island, called *Nun's Island*,
perhaps from an ancient convent. Here is said to have
been dug the stone that was used in the buildings of *Icolmkill*.
Whether it is now inhabited we could not stay to inquire.

At last we came to *Icolmkill*, but found no convenience
for landing. Our boat could not be forced very near the
dry ground, and our Highlanders carried us over the water.
20 We were now treading that illustrious Island, which was
once the luminary of the *Caledonian* regions, whence savage
clans and roving barbarians derived the benefits of knowledge, and the blessings of religion. To abstract the mind
from all local emotion would be impossible, if it were
endeavoured, and would be foolish, if it were possible.
Whatever withdraws us from the power of our senses ;
whatever makes the past, the distant, or the future predominate over the present, advances us in the dignity of
thinking beings. Far from me and from my friends, be
30 such frigid philosophy as may conduct us indifferent and
unmoved over any ground which has been dignified by
wisdom, bravery, or virtue. That man is little to be envied,
whose patriotism would not gain force upon the plain of
Marathon, or whose piety would not grow warmer among
the ruins of *Iona !*

From *PREFACES, BIOGRAPHICAL AND CRITICAL, TO THE WORKS OF THE ENGLISH POETS*

Published 1779–1781 ; *printed from the edition revised by the author in* 1783.

MILTON

IT is justly remarked by Addison, that this poem has, by the nature of its subject, the advantage above all others, that it is universally and perpetually interesting. All mankind will, through all ages, bear the same relation to Adam and to Eve, and must partake of that good and evil which extend to themselves. . . .

The questions, whether the action of the poem be strictly *one*, whether the poem can be properly termed *heroic*, and who is the hero, are raised by such readers as draw their principles of judgement rather from books than from reason. 10 Milton, though he entitled *Paradise Lost* only a *poem*, yet calls it himself *heroic song*. Dryden, petulantly and indecently, denies the heroism of Adam, because he was overcome ; but there is no reason why the hero should not be unfortunate, except established practice, since success and virtue do not go necessarily together. Cato is the hero of Lucan ; but Lucan's authority will not be suffered by Quintilian to decide. However, if success be necessary, Adam's deceiver was at last crushed ; Adam was restored to his Maker's favour, and therefore may 20 securely resume his human rank.

After the scheme and fabric of the poem, must be considered its component parts, the sentiments and the diction.

The *sentiments*, as expressive of manners, or appropriated to characters, are, for the greater part, unexceptionally just. Splendid passages, containing lessons of morality, or precepts of prudence, occur seldom. Such is the original formation of this poem, that as it admits no human manners till the Fall, it can give little assistance to human conduct. Its end is to raise the thoughts above sublunary cares or pleasures. Yet the praise of that fortitude, with which Abdiel maintained his singularity of virtue against the scorn of multitudes, may be accommodated to all times ; and Raphael's reproof of Adam's curiosity after the planetary motions, with the answer returned by Adam, may be confidently opposed to any rule of life which any poet has delivered.

The thoughts which are occasionally called forth in the progress, are such as could only be produced by an imagination in the highest degree fervid and active, to which materials were supplied by incessant study and unlimited curiosity. The heat of Milton's mind might be said to sublimate his learning, to throw off into his work the spirit of science, unmingled with its grosser parts.

He had considered creation in its whole extent, and his descriptions are therefore learned. He had accustomed his imagination to unrestrained indulgence, and his conceptions therefore were extensive. The characteristic quality of his poem is sublimity. He sometimes descends to the elegant, but his element is the great. He can occasionally invest himself with grace ; but his natural port is gigantic loftiness.[1] He can please when pleasure is required ; but it is his peculiar power to astonish.

He seems to have been well acquainted with his own genius, and to know what it was that Nature had bestowed upon him more bountifully than upon others ; the power of displaying the vast, illuminating the splendid, enforcing

---

[1] Algarotti terms it *gigantesca sublimità Miltonièna.*

the awful, darkening the gloomy, and aggravating the dreadful : he therefore chose a subject on which too much could not be said, on which he might tire his fancy without the censure of extravagance.

The appearances of nature, and the occurrences of life, did not satiate his appetite of greatness. To paint things as they are, requires a minute attention, and employs the memory rather than the fancy. Milton's delight was to sport in the wide regions of possibility ; reality was a scene too narrow for his mind. He sent his faculties out upon discovery, into worlds where only imagination can travel, and delighted to form new modes of existence, and furnish sentiment and action to superior beings, to trace the counsels of hell, or accompany the choirs of heaven.

D R Y D E N

Criticism, either didactick or defensive, occupies almost all his prose, except those pages which he has devoted to his patrons ; but none of his prefaces were ever thought tedious. They have not the formality of a settled style, in which the first half of the sentence betrays the other. The clauses are never balanced, nor the periods modelled ; every word seems to drop by chance, though it falls into its proper place. Nothing is cold or languid ; the whole is airy, animated, and vigorous ; what is little, is gay ; what is great, is splendid. He may be thought to mention himself too frequently ; but while he forces himself upon our esteem, we cannot refuse him to stand high in his own. Every thing is excused by the play of images and the spriteliness of expression. Though all is easy, nothing is feeble ; though all seems careless, there is nothing harsh ; and though, since his earlier works, more than a century has passed, they have nothing yet uncouth or obsolete.

He who writes much, will not easily escape a manner,

such a recurrence of particular modes as may be easily noted. Dryden is always *another and the same*, he does not exhibit a second time the same elegances in the same form, nor appears to have any art other than that of expressing with clearness what he thinks with vigour. His style could not easily be imitated, either seriously or ludicrously ; for, being always equable and always varied, it has no prominent or discriminative characters. The beauty who is totally free from disproportion of parts and features, 10 cannot be ridiculed by an overcharged resemblance.

From his prose, however, Dryden derives only his accidental and secondary praise ; the veneration with which his name is pronounced by every cultivator of English literature, is paid to him as he refined the language, improved the sentiments, and tuned the numbers of English Poetry.

*   *   *   *   *   *   *

Absalom and Achitophel is a work so well known, that particular criticism is superfluous. If it be considered as a poem political and controversial, it will be found to 20 comprise all the excellences of which the subject is susceptible ; acrimony of censure, elegance of praise, artful delineation of characters, variety and vigour of sentiment, happy turns of language, and pleasing harmony of numbers ; and all these raised to such a height as can scarcely be found in any other English composition.

It is not, however, without faults ; some lines are inelegant or improper, and too many are irreligiously licentious. The original structure of the poem was defective ; allegories drawn to great length will always break ; 30 Charles could not run continually parallel with David.

The subject had likewise another inconvenience : it admitted little imagery or description, and a long poem of mere sentiments easily becomes tedious ; though all the parts are forcible, and every line kindles new rapture, the reader, if not relieved by the interposition of something that sooths the fancy, grows weary of admiration, and defers the rest.

As an approach to historical truth was necessary, the action and catastrophe were not in the poet's power ; there is therefore an unpleasing disproportion between the beginning and the end. We are alarmed by a faction formed out of many sects various in their principles, but agreeing in their purpose of mischief, formidable for their numbers, and strong by their supports, while the king's friends are few and weak. The chiefs on either part are set forth to view ; but when expectation is at the height, the king makes a speech, and

> Henceforth a series of new times began.

Who can forbear to think of an enchanted castle, with a wide moat and lofty battlements, walls of marble and gates of brass, which vanishes at once into air, when the destined knight blows his horn before it ?

* * * * * * *

Next to argument, his delight was in wild and daring sallies of sentiment, in the irregular and excentrick violence of wit. He delighted to tread upon the brink of meaning, where light and darkness begin to mingle ; to approach the precipice of absurdity, and hover over the abyss of unideal vacancy. This inclination sometimes produced nonsense, which he knew ; as,

> Move swiftly, sun, and fly a lover's pace,
> Leave weeks and months behind thee in thy race.
> > Amariel flies
> To guard thee from the demons of the air ;
> My flaming sword above them to display,
> All keen, and ground upon the edge of day.

And sometimes it issued in absurdities, of which perhaps he was not conscious :

> Then we upon our orb's last verge shall go,
>   And see the ocean leaning on the sky;
> From thence our rolling neighbours we shall know,
>   And on the lunar world securely pry.

These lines have no meaning; but may we not say, in imitation of Cowley on another book,

> 'Tis so like *sense* 'twill serve the turn as well?

*   *   *   *   *   *   *

Of such selection there is no end. I will add only a few more passages; of which the first, though it may perhaps not be quite clear in prose, is not too obscure for poetry, as the meaning that it has is noble:

> No, there is a necessity in Fate,
> Why still the brave bold man is fortunate;
> He keeps his object ever full in sight,
> And that assurance holds him firm and right;
> True, 'tis a narrow way that leads to bliss,
> But right before there is no precipice;
> Fear makes men look aside, and so their footing miss.

*   *   *   *   *   *   *

Of Dryden's works it was said by Pope, that *he could select from them better specimens of every mode of poetry than any other English writer could supply*. Perhaps no nation ever produced a writer that enriched his language with such variety of models. To him we owe the improvement, perhaps the completion of our metre, the refinement of our language, and much of the correctness of our sentiments. By him we were taught *sapere & fari*, to think naturally and express forcibly. Though Davis has reasoned in rhyme before him, it may be perhaps maintained that he was the first who joined argument with poetry. He shewed us the true bounds of a translator's liberty. What was said of Rome, adorned by Augustus, may be applied by an easy metaphor to English poetry embellished by Dryden, *lateritiam invenit, marmoream reliquit,* he found it brick, and he left it marble.

EDMUND SMITH

For the power of communicating these minute memorials,
I am indebted to my conversation with Gilbert Walmsley,
late register of the ecclesiastical court of Litchfield. . . .

Of Gilbert Walmsley, thus presented to my mind, let
me indulge myself in the remembrance. I knew him very
early ; he was one of the first friends that literature
procured me, and I hope that at least my gratitude made me
worthy of his notice.

He was of an advanced age, and I was only not a boy ;
yet he never received my notions with contempt. He was
a Whig, with all the virulence and malevolence of his
party ; yet difference of opinion did not keep us apart.
I honoured him, and he endured me.

He had mingled with the gay world, without exemption
from its vices or its follies, but had never neglected the
cultivation of his mind ; his belief of Revelation was
unshaken ; his learning preserved his principles ; he grew
first regular, and then pious.

His studies had been so various, that I am not able to
name a man of equal knowledge. His acquaintance with
books was great ; and what he did not immediately know,
he could at least tell where to find. Such was his amplitude
of learning, and such his copiousness of communication,
that it may be doubted whether a day now passes in which
I have not some advantage from his friendship.

At this man's table I enjoyed many chearful and instructive hours, with companions such as are not often found ;
with one who has lengthened, and one who has gladdened
life ; with Dr. James, whose skill in physick will be long
remembered ; and with David Garrick, whom I hoped to
have gratified with this character of our common friend :
but what are the hopes of man ! I am disappointed by that
stroke of death, which has eclipsed the gaiety of nations,
and impoverished the publick stock of harmless pleasure.

POPE

He professed to have learned his poetry from Dryden, whom, whenever an opportunity was presented, he praised through his whole life with unvaried liberality ; and perhaps his character may receive some illustration, if he be compared with his master.

Integrity of understanding and nicety of discernment were not allotted in a less proportion to Dryden than to Pope. The rectitude of Dryden's mind was sufficiently shewn by the dismission of his poetical prejudices, and the
10 rejection of unnatural thoughts and rugged numbers. But Dryden never desired to apply all the judgement that he had. He wrote, and professed to write, merely for the people ; and when he pleased others, he contented himself. He spent no time in struggles to rouse latent powers ; he never attempted to make that better which was already good, nor often to mend what he must have known to be faulty. He wrote, as he tells us, with very little consideration ; when occasion or necessity called upon him, he poured out what the present moment happened to supply,
20 and, when once it had passed the press, ejected it from his mind ; for when he had no pecuniary interest, he had no further solicitude.

Pope was not content to satisfy ; he desired to excel, and therefore always endeavoured to do his best : he did not court the candour, but dared the judgement of his reader, and, expecting no indulgence from others, he shewed none to himself. He examined lines and words with minute and punctilious observation, and retouched every part with indefatigable diligence, till he had left nothing to be
30 forgiven.

For this reason he kept his pieces very long in his hands, while he considered and reconsidered them. The only poems which can be supposed to have been written with such regard to the times as might hasten their publication, were the two satires of *Thirty-eight*; of which Dodsley told me, that they were brought to him by the author, that they might be fairly copied. 'Almost every line,' he said, ' was then written twice over ; I gave him a clean transcript, ' which he sent some time afterwards to me for the press, ' with almost every line written twice over a second time.'

His declaration, that his care for his works ceased at their publication, was not strictly true. His parental attention never abandoned them ; what he found amiss 10 in the first edition, he silently corrected in those that followed. He appears to have revised the *Iliad*, and freed it from some of its imperfections ; and the *Essay on Criticism* received many improvements after its first appearance. It will seldom be found that he altered without adding clearness, elegance, or vigour. Pope had perhaps the judgement of Dryden ; but Dryden certainly wanted the diligence of Pope.

In acquired knowledge, the superiority must be allowed to Dryden, whose education was more scholastick, and who 20 before he became an author had been allowed more time for study, with better means of information. His mind has a larger range, and he collects his images and illustrations from a more extensive circumference of science. Dryden knew more of man in his general nature, and Pope in his local manners. The notions of Dryden were formed by comprehensive speculation, and those of Pope by minute attention. There is more dignity in the knowledge of Dryden, and more certainty in that of Pope.

Poetry was not the sole praise of either ; for both 30 excelled likewise in prose ; but Pope did not borrow his prose from his predecessor. The style of Dryden is capricious and varied, that of Pope is cautious and uniform ; Dryden obeys the motions of his own mind, Pope constrains his mind to his own rules of composition. Dryden is sometimes vehement and rapid ; Pope is always smooth, uniform, and gentle. Dryden's page is a natural field, rising into inequalities, and diversified by the varied exuberance of abundant vegetation ; Pope's is a velvet lawn, shaven by the scythe, and levelled by the roller.

Of genius, that power which constitutes a poet ; that quality without which judgement is cold and knowledge is inert ; that energy which collects, combines, amplifies and animates ; the superiority must, with some hesitation, be ₁₀ allowed to Dryden. It is not to be inferred that of this poetical vigour Pope had only a little, because Dryden had more ; for every other writer since Milton must give place to Pope ; and even of Dryden it must be said, that if he has brighter paragraphs, he has not better poems. Dryden's performances were always hasty, either excited by some external occasion, or extorted by domestick necessity ; he composed without consideration, and published without correction. What his mind could supply at call, or gather in one excursion, was all that he sought, and all that he ₂₀ gave. The dilatory caution of Pope enabled him to condense his sentiments, to multiply his images, and to accumulate all that study might produce, or chance might supply. If the flights of Dryden therefore are higher, Pope continues longer on the wing. If of Dryden's fire the blaze is brighter, of Pope's the heat is more regular and constant. Dryden often surpasses expectation, and Pope never falls below it. Dryden is read with frequent astonishment, and Pope with perpetual delight.

This parallel will, I hope, when it is well considered, be ₃₀ found just ; and if the reader should suspect me, as I suspect myself, of some partial fondness for the memory of Dryden, let him not too hastily condemn me ; for meditation and enquiry may, perhaps, shew him the reasonableness of my determination.

* * * * * * *

To the praises which have been accumulated on *The Rape of the Lock* by readers of every class, from the critick to the waiting-maid, it is difficult to make any addition. Of that which is universally allowed to be the most attractive of all ludicrous compositions, let it rather be now enquired from what sources the power of pleasing is derived.

Dr. Warburton, who excelled in critical perspicacity, has remarked that the preternatural agents are very happily adapted to the purposes of the poem. The heathen deities can no longer gain attention : we should have turned away from a contest between Venus and Diana. The employment of allegorical persons always excites conviction of its own absurdity ; they may produce effects, but cannot conduct actions ; when the phantom is put in motion, it dissolves ; thus *Discord* may raise a mutiny, but *Discord* cannot conduct a march, nor besiege a town. Pope brought into view a new race of Beings, with powers and passions proportionate to their operation. The sylphs and gnomes act at the toilet and the tea-table, what more terrifick and more powerful phantoms perform on the stormy ocean, or the field of battle, they give their proper help, and do their proper mischief.

Pope is said, by an objector, not to have been the inventer of this petty nation ; a charge which might with more justice have been brought against the author of the *Iliad*, who doubtless adopted the religious system of his country ; for what is there but the names of his agents which Pope has not invented ? Has he not assigned them characters and operations never heard of before ? Has he not, at least, given them their first poetical existence ? If this is not sufficient to denominate his work original, nothing original ever can be written.

In this work are exhibited, in a very high degree, the two most engaging powers of an author. New things are made familiar, and familiar things are made new. A race of aerial people, never heard of before, is presented to us in a manner so clear and easy, that the reader seeks for no further information, but immediately mingles with his new acquaintance, adopts their interests, and attends their pursuits, loves a sylph, and detests a gnome.

That familiar things are made new, every paragraph will prove. The subject of the poem is an event below the common incidents of common life; nothing real is intro-
10 duced that is not seen so often as to be no longer regarded, yet the whole detail of a female-day is here brought before us invested with so much art of decoration, that, though nothing is disguised, every thing is striking, and we feel all the appetite of curiosity for that from which we have a thousand times turned fastidiously away.

*   *   *   *   *   *

The *Essay on Man* was a work of great labour and long consideration, but certainly not the happiest of Pope's performances. The subject is perhaps not very proper for poetry, and the poet was not sufficiently master of his
20 subject; metaphysical morality was to him a new study, he was proud of his acquisitions, and, supposing himself master of great secrets, was in haste to teach what he had not learned. Thus he tells us, in the first Epistle, that from the nature of the Supreme Being may be deduced an order of beings such as mankind, because Infinite Excellence can do only what is best. He finds out that these beings must be *somewhere*, and that *all the question is whether man be in a wrong place*. Surely if, according to the poet's Leibnitian reasoning, we may infer that man ought to be,
30 only because he is, we may allow that his place is the right place, because he has it. Supreme Wisdom is not less infallible in disposing than in creating. But what is meant by *somewhere* and *place*, and *wrong place*, it had been vain to ask Pope, who probably had never asked himself.

Having exalted himself into the chair of wisdom, he tells us much that every man knows, and much that he does not know himself ; that we see but little, and that the order of the universe is beyond our comprehension ; an opinion not very uncommon ; and that there is a chain of subordinate beings *from infinite to nothing*, of which himself and his readers are equally ignorant. But he gives us one comfort, which, without his help, he supposes unattainable, in the position *that though we are fools, yet God is wise.*

This Essay affords an egregious instance of the pre- 10 dominance of genius, the dazzling splendour of imagery, and the seductive powers of eloquence. Never were penury of knowledge and vulgarity of sentiment so happily disguised. The reader feels his mind full, though he learns nothing ; and when he meets it in its new array, no longer knows the talk of his mother and his nurse. When these wonder-working sounds sink into sense, and the doctrine of the Essay, disrobed of its ornaments, is left to the powers of its naked excellence, what shall we discover ? That we are, in comparison with our Creator, very weak 20 and ignorant ; that we do not uphold the chain of existence, and that we could not make one another with more skill than we are made. We may learn yet more ; that the arts of human life were copied from the instinctive opera- tions of other animals ; that if the world be made for man, it may be said that man was made for geese. To these profound principles of natural knowledge are added some moral instructions equally new ; that self-interest, well understood, will produce social concord ; that men are mutual gainers by mutual benefits ; that evil is sometimes 30 balanced by good ; that human advantages are unstable and fallacious, of uncertain duration, and doubtful effect ; that our true honour is, not to have a great part, but to act it well : that virtue only is our own ; and that happi- ness is always in our power.

Surely a man of no very comprehensive search may venture to say that he has heard all this before; but it was never till now recommended by such a blaze of embellishment, or such sweetness of melody. The vigorous contraction of some thoughts, the luxuriant amplification of others, the incidental illustrations, and sometimes the dignity, sometimes the softness of the verses, enchain philosophy, suspend criticism, and oppress judgement by overpowering pleasure.

GRAY

10 IN the character of his *Elegy* I rejoice to concur with the common reader; for by the common sense of readers uncorrupted with literary prejudices, after all the refinements of subtilty and the dogmatism of learning, must be finally decided all claim to poetical honours. The *Church-yard* abounds with images which find a mirrour in every mind, and with sentiments to which every bosom returns an echo. The four stanzas beginning *Yet even these bones,* are to me original: I have never seen the notions in any other place; yet he that reads them here, persuades 20 himself that he has always felt them. Had Gray written often thus, it had been vain to blame, and useless to praise him.

Selections from

J O H N S O N ' S

Occasional Writings

&

Letters

On the

BRAVERY

of the

ENGLISH COMMON SOLDIERS

Published 1767

BY those who have compared the military genius of
the *English* with that of the *French* nation, it is remarked,
that *the French officers will always lead, if the soldiers will
follow ;* and that *the English soldiers will always follow, if
their officers will lead.*

In all pointed sentences, some degree of accuracy must
be sacrificed to conciseness ; and, in this comparison, our
officers seem to lose what our soldiers gain. I know not
any reason for supposing that the *English* officers are less
willing than the *French* to lead ; but it is, I think, universally allowed, that the *English* soldiers are more willing
to follow. Our nation may boast, beyond any other people
in the world, of a kind of epidemick bravery, diffused
equally through all its ranks. We can shew a peasantry
of heroes, and fill our armies with clowns, whose courage
may vie with that of their general.

There may be some pleasure in tracing the causes of this
plebeian magnanimity. The qualities which commonly
make an army formidable, are long habits of regularity,
great exactness of discipline, and great confidence in the
commander. Regularity may, in time, produce a kind of
mechanical obedience to signals and commands, like that
which the perverse *Cartesians* impute to animals ; discipline may impress such an awe upon the mind, that any

danger shall be less dreaded than the danger of punishment ; and confidence in the wisdom or fortune of the general, may induce the soldiers to follow him blindly to the most dangerous enterprise.

What may be done by discipline and regularity, may be seen in the troops of the *Russian* empress and *Prussian* monarch. We find that they may be broken without confusion, and repulsed without flight.

But the *English* troops have none of these requisites in
10 any eminent degree. Regularity is by no means part of their character : they are rarely exercised, and therefore shew very little dexterity in their evolutions as bodies of men, or in the manual use of their weapons as individuals ; they neither are thought by others, nor by themselves, more active or exact than their enemies, and therefore derive none of their courage from such imaginary superiority.

The manner in which they are dispersed in quarters over the country during times of peace, naturally produces laxity of discipline : they are very little in sight of their
20 officers ; and, when they are not engaged in the slight duty of the guard, are suffered to live every man his own way.

The equality of *English* privileges, the impartiality of our laws, the freedom of our tenures, and the prosperity of our trade, dispose us very little to reverence of superiours. It is not to any great esteem of the officers that the *English* soldier is indebted for his spirit in the hour of battle ; for perhaps it does not often happen that he thinks much better of his leader than of himself. The *French* count,
30 who has lately published the *Art of War*, remarks how much soldiers are animated, when they see all their dangers shared by those who were born to be their masters, and whom they consider as beings of a different rank. The *Englishman* despises such motives of courage : he was born without a master ; and looks not on any man, however dignified by

lace or titles, as deriving from nature any claims to his respect, or inheriting any qualities superiour to his own.

There are some, perhaps, who would imagine that every *Englishman* fights better than the subjects of absolute governments, because he has more to defend. But what has the *English* more than the *French* soldier ? Property they are both commonly without. Liberty is, to the lowest rank of every nation, little more than the choice of working or starving ; and this choice is, I suppose, equally allowed in every country. The *English* soldier seldom has 10 his head very full of the constitution ; nor has there been, for more than a century, any war that put the property or liberty of a single *Englishman* in danger.

Whence then is the courage of the *English* vulgar ? It proceeds, in my opinion, from that dissolution of dependence which obliges every man to regard his own character. While every man is fed by his own hands, he has no need of any servile arts ; he may always have wages for his labour ; and is no less necessary to his employer, than his employer is to him. While he looks for no protection from 20 others, he is naturally roused to be his own protector ; and having nothing to abate his esteem of himself, he consequently aspires to the esteem of others. Thus every man that crowds our streets is a man of honour, disdainful of obligation, impatient of reproach, and desirous of extending his reputation among those of his own rank ; and as courage is in most frequent use, the fame of courage is most eagerly pursued. From this neglect of subordination I do not deny that some inconveniencies may from time to time proceed : the power of the law does not always sufficiently 30 supply the want of reverence, or maintain the proper distinction between different ranks ; but good and evil will grow up in this world together ; and they who complain, in peace, of the insolence of the populace, must remember, that their insolence in peace is bravery in war.

DEDICATION

of

A Commentary with Notes on the four Evangelists
and the Acts of the Apostles
by Zachary Pearce, Bishop of Rochester

Published 1777

TO THE KING

' SIR,—I presume to lay before your Majesty the last labours of a learned Bishop, who died in the toils and duties of his calling. He is now beyond the reach of all earthly honours and rewards ; and only the hope of inciting others to imitate him, makes it now fit to be remembered, that he enjoyed in his life the favour of your Majesty.

' The tumultuary life of Princes seldom permits them to survey the wide extent of national interest, without losing sight of private merit ; to exhibit qualities which may be imitated by the highest and the humblest of mankind ; and to be at once amiable and great.

' Such characters, if now and then they appear in history, are contemplated with admiration. May it be the ambition of all your subjects to make haste with their tribute of reverence : and as posterity may learn from your Majesty how Kings should live, may they learn, likewise, from your people, how they should be honoured. I am, may it please your Majesty, with the most profound respect, your Majesty's most dutiful and devoted

' Subject and Servant.'

Dedication of Sir JOSHUA REYNOLDS'S
Discourses to the Royal Academy (1778)

TO THE KING

THE regular progress of cultivated life is from necessaries to accommodations, from accommodations to ornaments. By your illustrious predecessors were established Marts for manufactures, and Colleges for science; but for the arts of elegance, those arts by which manufactures are embellished, and science is refined, to found an Academy was reserved for Your Majesty.

Had such patronage been without effect, there had been reason to believe that Nature had, by some insurmountable impediment, obstructed our proficiency; but the annual improvement of the Exhibitions which Your Majesty has been pleased to encourage, shows that only encouragement had been wanting.

To give advice to those who are contending for royal liberality, has been for some years the duty of my station in the Academy; and these Discourses hope for your Majesty's acceptance, as well-intended endeavours to incite that emulation which your notice has kindled, and direct those studies which your bounty has rewarded.

May it please your Majesty,
Your Majesty's
Most dutiful servant,
and most faithful subject,
JOSHUA REYNOLDS.

From JAMES BOSWELL'S
LIFE OF SAMUEL JOHNSON, LL.D.

Published 1791

(i) Letter to Lord Chesterfield

LORD CHESTERFIELD, to whom Johnson had paid the high compliment of addressing to his Lordship the *Plan* of his *Dictionary*, had behaved to him in such a manner as to excite his contempt and indignation. . . . He told me, that there never was any particular incident which produced a quarrel between Lord Chesterfield and him ; but that his Lordship's continued neglect was the reason why he resolved to have no connection with him. When the *Dictionary* was upon the eve of publication, Lord Chester-
10 field, who, it is said, had flattered himself with expectations that Johnson would dedicate the work to him, attempted, in a courtly manner, to sooth, and insinuate himself with the Sage, conscious, as it should seem, of the cold indifference with which he had treated its learned authour ; and further attempted to conciliate him, by writing two papers in *The World*, in recommendation of the work ; and it must be confessed, that they contain some studied compliments, so finely turned, that if there had been no previous offence, it is probable that Johnson would have been highly
20 delighted. Praise, in general, was pleasing to him ; but by praise from a man of rank and elegant accomplishments, he was peculiarly gratified.

This courtly device failed of its effect. Johnson, who thought that 'all was false and hollow', despised the honeyed words, and was even indignant that Lord Chesterfield should, for a moment, imagine that he could be the dupe of such an artifice. His expression to me concerning

Lord Chesterfield, upon this occasion, was, ' Sir, after making great professions, he had, for many years, taken no notice of me; but when my *Dictionary* was coming out, he fell a scribbling in *The World* about it. Upon which, I wrote him a letter expressed in civil terms, but such as might shew him that I did not mind what he said or wrote, and that I had done with him.'

This is that celebrated letter of which so much has been said, and about which curiosity has been so long excited, without being gratified. I for many years solicited Johnson 10 to favour me with a copy of it, that so excellent a composition might not be lost to posterity. He delayed from time to time to give it me ; till at last in 1781, when we were on a visit at Mr. Dilly's, at Southill in Bedfordshire, he was pleased to dictate it to me from memory. He afterwards found among his papers a copy of it, which he had dictated to Mr. Baretti, with its title and corrections, in his own handwriting. This he gave to Mr. Langton ; adding that if it were to come into print, he wished it to be from that copy. By Mr. Langton's kindness, I am enabled to enrich 20 my work with a perfect transcript of what the world has so eagerly desired to see.

' TO THE RIGHT HONOURABLE THE EARL OF CHESTERFIELD.

   ' MY LORD,   February 7, 1755.

    ' I have been lately informed, by the proprietor of *The World*, that two papers, in which my Dictionary is recommended to the publick, were written by your Lordship. To be so distinguished, is an honour, which, being very little accustomed to favours from the great, I know not well how to receive, or in what terms to acknowledge.   30

    ' When, upon some slight encouragement, I first visited your Lordship, I was overpowered, like the rest of mankind, by the enchantment of your address ; and could not forbear to wish that I might boast myself *Le vainqueur du vainqueur de ta terre* ;—that I might obtain that regard for which I saw the world contending ; but I found my attendance so little encouraged, that neither pride nor modesty would suffer me to continue it. When I had once addressed your Lordship in publick, I had exhausted all the art of pleasing which a retired and uncourtly scholar can possess. I had done all that I could ; and no man is well pleased to have his all neglected, be it ever so little.

'Seven years, my Lord, have now past, since I waited in your outward rooms, or was repulsed from your door ; during which time I have been pushing on my work through difficulties, of which it is useless to complain, and have brought it, at last, to the verge of publication, without one act of assistance, one word of encouragement, or one smile of favour. Such treatment I did not expect, for I never had a Patron before.

'The shepherd in Virgil grew at last acquainted with Love, and found him a native of the rocks.

'Is not a Patron, my Lord, one who looks with unconcern on a man struggling for life in the water, and, when he has reached ground, encumbers him with help ? The notice which you have been pleased to take of my labours, had it been early, had been kind ; but it has been delayed till I am indifferent, and cannot enjoy it ; till I am solitary, and cannot impart it ; till I am known, and do not want it. I hope it is no very cynical asperity not to confess obligations where no benefit has been received, or to be unwilling that the Publick should consider me as owing that to a Patron, which Providence has enabled me to do for myself.

'Having carried on my work thus far with so little obligation to any favourer of learning, I shall not be disappointed though I should conclude it, if less be possible, with less ; for I have been long wakened from that dream of hope, in which I once boasted myself with so much exultation, my Lord, your Lordship's most humble, most obedient servant,   'SAM. JOHNSON.'

(ii) Johnson on *Ossian*

'TO JAMES BOSWELL, ESQ.

'MY DEAR BOSWELL,—I am surprized that, knowing as you do the disposition of your countrymen to tell lies in favour of each other, you can be at all affected by any reports that circulate among them. Macpherson never in his life offered me a sight of any original or of any evidence of any kind ; but thought only of intimidating me by noise and threats, till my last answer,—that I would not be deterred from detecting what I thought a cheat, by the menaces of a ruffian—put an end to our correspondence.   10

'The state of the question is this. He, and Dr. Blair, whom I consider as deceived, say, that he copied the poem from old manuscripts. His copies, if he had them, and I believe him to have none, are nothing. Where are the manuscripts ? They can be shewn if they exist, but they were never shewn. *De non existentibus et non apparentibus*, says our law, *eadem est ratio*. No man has a claim to credit upon his own word, when better evidence, if he had it, may be easily produced. But, so far as we can find, the Erse language was never written till very lately for the purposes of 20 religion. A nation that cannot write, or a language that was never written, has no manuscripts.

'But whatever he has he never offered to show. If old manuscripts should now be mentioned, I should, unless there were more evidence than can be easily had, suppose them another proof of Scotch conspiracy in national falsehood.

'Do not censure the expression ; you know it to be true.

.   .   .   .

I am, Sir, your most humble servant,
      'February 7, 1775.'   'SAM. JOHNSON.'

What words were used by Mr. Macpherson in his letter to
the venerable Sage, I have never heard ; but they are generally said to have been of a nature very different from the
language of literary contest.   Dr. Johnson's answer appeared in the news-papers of the day, and has since been
frequently re-published ; but not with perfect accuracy.
I give it as dictated to me by himself, written down in his
presence, and authenticated by a note in his own hand-writ-
ing, ' *This, I think, is a true copy.*'

10   ' MR. JAMES MACPHERSON,—I received your foolish and
impudent letter.   Any violence offered me I shall do my best
to repel ; and what I cannot do for myself, the law shall do
for me.   I hope I shall never be deterred from detecting
what I think a cheat, by the menaces of a ruffian.

' What would you have me retract ?   I thought your book
an imposture ; I think it an imposture still.   For this opinion I have given my reasons to the publick, which I here dare
you to refute.   Your rage I defy.   Your abilities, since your
Homer, are not so formidable ; and what I hear of your
20 morals, inclines me to pay regard not to what you shall say,
but to what you shall prove.   You may print this if you will.

' SAM. JOHNSON.'

Private Letters.

To George Strahan.

Dear George,

To give pain ought always to be painful, and I am sorry that I have been the occasion of any uneasiness to you, to whom I hope never to [do] any thing but for your benefit or your pleasure. Your uneasiness was without any reason on your part, as you had written with sufficient frequency to me, and I had only neglected to answer them, because as nothing new had been proposed to your study, no new direction or incitement could be offered you. 10 But if it had happened that you had omitted what you did not omit, and that I had for an hour, or a week, or a much longer time, thought myself put out of your mind by something to which presence gave that prevalence, which presence will sometimes give even where there is the most prudence and experience, you are not to imagine that my friendship is light enough to be blown away by the first cross blast, or that my regard or kindness hangs by so slender a hair as to be broken off by the unfelt weight of a petty offence. I love you, and hope to love you long. 20 You have hitherto done nothing to diminish my good will, and though you had done much more than you have supposed imputed to you, my good will would not have been diminished.

I write thus largely on this suspicion, which you have suffered to enter your mind, because in youth we are apt to be too rigorous in our expectations, and to suppose that the duties of life are to be performed with unfailing exactness and regularity; but in our progress through life we are forced to abate much of our demands, and to take friends 30 such as we can find them, not as we would make them.

These concessions every wise man is more ready to

make to others, as he knows that he shall often want them
for himself ; and when he remembers how often he fails in
the observance or cultivation of his best friends, is willing
to suppose that his friends may in their turn neglect him,
without any intention to offend him.

When therefore it shall happen, as happen it will, that
you or I have disappointed the expectation of the other,
you are not to suppose that you have lost me, or that
I intended to lose you ; nothing will remain but to repair
10 the fault, and to go on as if it never had been committed.

I am, Sir,

Your affectionate servant,

SAM : JOHNSON.

Thursday, July 14, 1763.

To MRS. THRALE.

MADAM,   Lichfield, August 14, 1769.

I set out on Thursday morning, and found my companion, to whom I was very much a stranger, more agreeable than I expected. We went cheerfully forward, and
20 passed the night at Coventry. We came in late, and went
out early ; and therefore I did not send for my cousin Tom ;
but I design to make him some amends for the omission.

Next day we came early to Lucy, who was, I believe,
glad to see us. She had saved her best gooseberries upon
the tree for me ; and, as Steele says. *I was neither too
proud nor too wise* to gather them. I have rambled a very
little *inter fontes et flumina nota,* but I am not yet well.
They have cut down the trees in George Lane. Evelyn,
in his book of Forest Trees, tells us of wicked men that
30 cut down trees, and never prospered afterwards ; yet
nothing has deterred these audacious aldermen from
violating the Hamadryads of George Lane. As an impartial
traveller I must however tell, that in Stow-street, where

I left a draw-well, I have found a pump; but the lading-well in this ill-fated George Lane lies shamefully neglected.

I am going to-day or to-morrow to Ashbourne; but I am at a loss how I shall get back in time to London. Here are only chance coaches, so that there is no certainty of a place. If I do not come, let it not hinder your journey. I can be but a few days behind you; and I will follow in the Brighthelmstone coach. But I hope to come.

I took care to tell Miss Porter, that I have got another Lucy. I hope she is well. Tell Mrs. Salusbury, that I beg 10 her stay at Streatham, for little Lucy's sake.

> I am, &c.,
> SAM: JOHNSON.

To Mrs. Thrale.

DEAR MADAM,   Ashbourne, July 3, 1771.

Last Saturday I came to Ashbourne; the dangers or the pleasures of the journey I have at present no disposition to recount; else might I paint the beauties of my native plains; might I tell of ' the smiles of nature, and the charms of art:' else might I relate how I crossed the 20 Staffordshire canal, one of the great efforts of human labour, and human contrivance; which, from the bridge on which I viewed it, passed away on either side, and loses itself in distant regions, uniting waters that nature had divided, and dividing lands which nature had united. I might tell how these reflections fermented in my mind till the chaise stopped at Ashbourne, at Ashbourne in the Peak. Let not the barren name of the Peak terrify you; I have never wanted strawberries and cream. The great bull has no disease but age. I hope in time to be like the 30 great bull; and hope you will be like him too a hundred years hence.   I am, &c.,

> SAM: JOHNSON.

To Mrs. Thrale.

[Ashbourne, July 1775.]

Now, thinks my dearest Mistress to herself, sure I am at last gone too far to be pestered every post with a letter : he knows that people go into the country to be at quiet ; he knows too that when I have once told the story of Ralph, the place where I am affords me nothing that I shall delight to tell, or he will wish to be told ; he knows how troublesome it is to write letters about nothing ; and he 10 knows that he does not love trouble himself, and therefore ought not to force it upon others.

But, dearest Lady, you may see once more how little knowledge influences practice, notwithstanding all this knowledge, you see, here is a letter.

Every body says the prospect of harvest is uncommonly delightful ; but this has been so long the Summer talk, and has been so often contradicted by Autumn, that I do not suffer it to lay much hold on my mind. Our gay prospects have now for many years together ended in 20 melancholy retrospects. Yet I am of opinion that there is much corn upon the ground. Every dear year encourages the farmer to sow more and more, and favourable seasons will be sent at last. Let us hope that they will be sent now.

The Doctor and Frank are gone to see the hay. It was cut on Saturday, and yesterday was well wetted ; but to day has its fill of sunshine. I hope the hay at Streatham was plentiful, and had good weather.

Our lawn is as you left it, only the pool is so full of mud 30 that the water-fowl have left it. Here are many calves, who, I suppose, all expect to be great bulls and cows.

Yesterday I saw Mrs. Diot at church, and shall drink tea with her some afternoon.

.   .   .   .

You will now find the advantage of having made one at the regatta. You will carry with you the importance of a publick personage, and enjoy a superiority which, having been only local and accidental, will not be regarded with malignity. You have a subject by which you can gratify general curiosity, and amuse your company without bewildering them. You can keep the vocal machine in motion, without those seeming paradoxes that are sure to disgust ; without that temerity of censure which is sure to provoke enemies ; and that exuberance of flattery which experience has found to make no friends. It is the good of publick life that it supplies agreeable topicks and general conversation. Therefore wherever you are, and whatever you see, talk not of the Punick war ; nor of the depravity of human nature ; nor of the slender motives of human actions ; nor of the difficulty of finding employment or pleasure ; but talk, and talk, and talk of the regatta, and keep the rest for, dearest Madam,

Your, &c.,

SAM : JOHNSON. 20

TO MRS. THRALE.

DEAR MADAM,   London, July 8, 1784.
    What you have done, however I may lament it, I have no pretence to resent, as it has not been injurious to me : I therefore breathe out one sigh more of tenderness, perhaps useless, but at least sincere.

I wish that God may grant you every blessing, that you may be happy in this world for its short continuance, and eternally happy in a better state ; and whatever I can contribute to your happiness I am very ready to repay, for that kindness which soothed twenty years of a life radically wretched.

Do not think slightly of the advice which I now presume

to offer. Prevail upon Mr. Piozzi to settle in England : you may live here with more dignity than in Italy, and with more security : your rank will be higher, and your fortune more under your own eye. I desire not to detail all my reasons, but every argument of prudence and interest is for England, and only some phantoms of imagination seduce you to Italy.

I am afraid however that my counsel is vain, yet I have eased my heart by giving it.

10 When Queen Mary took the resolution of sheltering herself in England, the Archbishop of St. Andrew's, attempting to dissuade her, attended on her journey ; and when they came to the irremeable stream that separated the two kingdoms, walked by her side into the water, in the middle of which he seized her bridle, and with earnestness proportioned to her danger and his own affection pressed her to return. The Queen went forward.—If the parallel reaches thus far, may it go no further.— The tears stand in my eyes.

20 I am going into Derbyshire, and hope to be followed by your good wishes, for I am, with great affection,

Your, &c.,

SAM : JOHNSON.

Any letters that come for me hither will be sent me.

NOTES

A

DICTIONARY

OF THE

ENGLISH LANGUAGE:

IN WHICH

The WORDS are deduced from their ORIGINALS,

AND

ILLUSTRATED in their DIFFERENT SIGNIFICATIONS

BY

EXAMPLES from the beft WRITERS.

TO WHICH ARE PREFIXED,

A HISTORY of the LANGUAGE,

AND

AN ENGLISH GRAMMAR.

BY SAMUEL JOHNSON, A. M.

IN TWO VOLUMES.

VOL. I.

Cum tabulis 'animum cenforis fumet honefti :
Audebit quæcunque parum fplendoris habebunt,
Et fine pondere erunt, et honore indigna ferentur.
Verba movere loco ; quamvis invita recedant,
Et verfentur adhuc intra penetralia Veftæ :
Obfcurata diu populo bonus eruet, atque
Proferet in lucem fpeciofa vocabula rerum,
Quæ prifcis memorata Catonibus atque Cethegis,
Nunc fitus informis premit et deferta vetuftas.   HOR.

LONDON,

Printed by W. STRAHAN,

For J. and P. KNAPTON ; T. and T. LONGMAN ; C. HITCH and L. HAWES ;
A. MILLAR; and R. and J. DODSLEY.

MDCCLV.

NOTES

The Vanity of Human Wishes (pp. 75–86).

The class of composition to which *London* and *The Vanity of Human Wishes* belong is thus described by Johnson in his account of Pope's Imitations of Horace :

' This mode of imitation, in which the ancients are familiarized, by adapting their sentiments to modern topicks, . . . was first practised in the reign of Charles the Second by Oldham and Rochester, at least I remember no instances more ancient. It is a kind of middle composition between translation and original design, which pleases when the thoughts are unexpectedly applicable, and the parallels lucky.'

Elsewhere in the *Life of Pope* he remarks that ' such imitation cannot give pleasure to common readers ; . . . the comparison requires knowledge of the original '. It is probably true that the *Vanity* is found most interesting by those who have the power, and take the trouble, to read it with Juvenal open before them ; but the poem is at the same time truly original, since it is an expression of the writer's own experience and conviction. It has, however, some obscurities which Johnson perhaps would not have allowed if the Latin had not been in his mind.

Many passages have only a general resemblance to their originals ; but the arrangement of the whole follows its model closely, and in the first edition the correspondence is indicated by foot-notes referring to the numbers of the lines in Juvenal. Readers to whom the Latin is inaccessible may profitably compare Johnson with Dryden's more literal translation of the Tenth Satire. But no translation can do justice to Juvenal's fierce and glowing rhetoric.

Only one edition of *The Vanity of Human Wishes* (the first, 1749) was published under Johnson's supervision. But the poem was included in Volume IV (first published 1755) of Dodsley's *Collection of Poems by Several Hands*, and in this version new readings made their appearance, some of which are certainly the author's own. I have generally followed the received text, which in the main follows Dodsley's ; but I have sometimes preferred the original reading, and I have restored throughout the initial capitals of nouns, as printed in the first edition.

The Argument may be thus summarized :

ll. 1–20. The Vanity of Human Wishes ; men pray for

Courage, for Eloquence, and especially for Wealth, and in so praying pray for their own destruction.

ll. 21–48. The Vanity of Wealth.

ll. 49–72. Invocation of Democritus ; the folly and corruption of public life.

ll. 73–134. The Vanity of Greatness ; the fall of Wolsey (Juvenal's Sejanus), and others.

ll. 135–74. The Vanity of Learning ; the Scholar's Life ; the fall of Laud (in Juvenal, Demosthenes and Cicero).

ll. 175–254. The Vanity of Conquest ; the fall of Charles of Sweden (Juvenal's Hannibal) ; of Xerxes, of Albert of Bavaria (in Juvenal, Xerxes, Alexander the Great).

ll. 255–318. The Vanity of Long Life ; the Miseries of Dotage.

ll. 319–42. The Vanity of Beauty.

ll. 343–68. Conclusion ; the proper objects of Prayer.

ll. 1, 2. It was remarked in an anonymous *Life* of Johnson, published in 1785, that the opening couplet is tautologous. This became a commonplace of romantic criticism ; it is repeated by Coleridge, Wordsworth, De Quincey, and even by Byron, who did not join in the general depreciation of Johnson current in his day.

l. 15. *Fate wings* : the construction is not obvious, but *Gift* and *Grace* seem to be appositional to *Wish,* not to *Dart.* Fate wings the destructive dart (as an arrow is *winged* with a feather) with every wish of its victim to shine, and with every gift that leads him to eminence, whether it be Courage or Eloquence.

ll. 17–20. Notice the arrangement *a b b a* (Courage, Elocution, Speaker, Fire), called by the ancient rhetoricians *Chiasmus,* from its supposed resemblance to the Greek letter *chi,* X.

l. 22. *Massacre of Gold* has been explained as ' plunder of the wealthy '. That this cannot be the meaning is clear from the Latin, which may be baldly translated thus : ' Courage and Eloquence bring many to destruction ; but far more are ruined by the wealth they have too anxiously amassed.' *Gold* therefore is here not the object of plunder, but itself the murderer : men commit crimes to grow rich, and become in turn the victims of others' avarice.

l. 34. *wealthy Traitor* : the first edition had *bonny Traytor,* in allusion to the Scottish Jacobites who were attainted for their part in the *Forty-Five.* They are commemorated in the well-known lines :

> Pity'd by gentle minds *Kilmarnock* died ;
> The brave, *Balmerino,* were on thy side.

l. 37. *The needy Traveller* : ' He who travels with empty pockets ', says Juvenal, ' may whistle in the robber's face.' But the wealthy Englishman in his carriage, like the wealthy

Roman in his litter, was exposed to very real danger. ' I don't make a visit without a blunderbuss,' writes Horace Walpole ; ' one might as well be invaded by the French.'

l. 39. *Does Envy seize thee ?* If the poor man's innocent happiness excites envy and *upbraids* a guilty conscience, all that need be done is to rid him of his poverty, and so of his peace of mind.

l. 45. *the Skies assail* : the metaphor is from the hunting-field, and *tainted* means no more than *scented*.

l. 48. *the gaping Heir* : Frederick, Prince of Wales, son of George II and father of George III, was on bad terms with the King, and in 1737 was forbidden the Court. He then lent his name to the Opposition, and kept a petty court of his own. He died in 1751, nine years before his father.

l. 49. *Democritus*, the ' laughing philosopher ' of antiquity. The sense of lines 53–62 is : even in the cities of ancient Greece, where life was simple, laborious, and uniform, Demo-critus found enough to laugh at in human absurdity ; how much more would he ' shake ' his sides if he could visit modern England, and witness the adulation of wealth, the insincerity of parliamentary debates, the foolish pomp of a Lord Mayor's Show, the changes produced by the fall of ministers, the travesty of justice in the law-courts.

l. 65. *were* is probably conditional, like *would'st* in l. 61, not past tense ; the *robes of pleasure*, &c., being those of England, not of Greece.

l. 72. *state* : not polity, but condition of life.

l. 76. *They mount* : the metaphor is from a sky-rocket.

l. 83. *descends the painted face* : Juvenal had described how on the fall of Sejanus, the favourite of the Emperor Tiberius, his statues were thrown down and melted by the populace which had once worshipped them.

l. 84. *Palladium* : the image of the goddess Pallas, which was fabled to have fallen from heaven into Troy, and upon which the safety of the city depended.

l. 91. *Britain*. Juvenal had deplored the degradation of the Roman people, who had resigned their imperial privileges and asked only for *panem et circenses* (*ludos*), bread-doles and races. Johnson contrasts the subservience and venality of the British electors with that resolute expression of the popular will which in the preceding century had dethroned kings, ruined ministers, and protected popular favourites.

l. 97. *septennial ale* : because the maximum duration of a Parliament was then (and until 1910) seven years.

l. 113. *At once is lost* : originally *Now drops at once* ; altered, doubtless, to avoid the ludicrous suggestion of ' Now drops . . . the glitt'ring Plate '.

l. 120. *his last Sighs* : Johnson is thinking of the speech at the end of the third act of *Henry VIII*. The original is in Holinshed : ' If I had served God as diligentlie as I have doone the king, he would not have given me over in my greie haires.'

l. 124. *richest Landlord* was altered to *wisest Justice*, but the change does not seem to be an improvement, and it may not have been Johnson's. A rich but obscure landlord may be tempted to leave the safety of the country (*Trent* indicating remoteness from the capital) and aspire to power (which can only be enjoyed on the banks of the Thames). *Wisest Justice* has been supposed to allude to Johnson's friend Gilbert Walmsley, registrar of the ecclesiastical court at Lichfield (for his character see p. 143). Lichfield is in the valley of the Trent ; but it is difficult to find any other point in the supposed allusion.

ll. 129–31. *Villiers* : George Villiers, first Duke of Buckingham, the favourite of James I and Charles I, assassinated in 1628. *Harley* : Robert Harley, first Earl of Oxford, the Tory minister of Queen Anne ; dismissed from favour in 1714. His closing years were made wretched by bodily pain. *Wentworth* : Thomas Wentworth, first Earl of Strafford, Charles I's minister, impeached by the Commons, and executed in 1641. *Hyde* : Edward Hyde, first Earl of Clarendon, Lord Chancellor under Charles II ; he was dismissed in 1667, and fled to France, where he wrote the famous *History of the Rebellion*.

l. 132. The order here is not ' chiastic ' as in 17–20 ; it was Hyde who was ' to Kings ally'd ' ; his daughter Anne married the Duke of York, afterwards James II, and was the mother of Queen Mary and Queen Anne.

l. 139. *Bodley's dome*. To those who are familiar with Oxford, this naturally suggests the Radcliffe Camera—a beautiful polygonal building surmounted by a dome. But in 1749 the Camera was only just completed. *Dome* means no more than *building*, and the reference is to the University Library, restored and endowed by Sir Thomas Bodley in 1600 and now universally known as the Bodleian Library.

l. 140. *Bacon's Mansion*. In Dodsley's Collection is the following foot-note : ' There is a tradition, that the study of friar Bacon, built on an arch over the bridge, will fall, when a man greater than Bacon shall pass under it.' The bridge was *Grand Pont*, now called *Folly Bridge*, one of the two which span the Thames at Oxford.

l. 160. *the Patron*. The first edition has *the Garret* ; Johnson substituted *Patron* ' after experiencing the uneasiness which Lord Chesterfield's fallacious patronage made him feel ' (Boswell). The Letter to Chesterfield (see p. 158) was written in February, and the revised version of the *Vanity* appeared in Dodsley's Collection in March, 1755.

l. 162. *the tardy Bust* : explained as referring to the bust of

Milton placed in Westminster Abbey in 1737; but Milton was not the only writer to whom this kind of tribute was paid when he had long been dead.

l. 164. *Galileo's* closing years were made wretched by blindness and other afflictions.

The allusion to *Lydiat* was obscure to Johnson's contemporaries, and explanations were printed in the *Gentleman's Magazine*. Thomas Lydiat, an Oxford scholar (1572–1646), was ranked very high by his contemporaries as a chronologist; but he was imprisoned for debt (like Johnson after him) and suffered for his political opinions.

l. 165. *last prize.* An eminent scholar was in those days often made a bishop. Learning's highest reward, therefore, might be the Archbishopric of Canterbury.

l. 168. *Laud* was not a conspicuously learned man, though he was an eminent patron of learning, particularly at Oxford, where he made the *Laudian Statutes* for the better government of the University, procured a charter for the University Press, and richly endowed the Bodleian with ancient manuscripts. Johnson's admiration was due in part to his political prejudices. For a more virulent display of the opposite prejudices see Macaulay's comments on these lines (p. 16).

l. 169. *From meaner minds.* The exaction of smaller penalties from lesser victims satisfied the persecutors.

l. 170. *sequester'd* = sequestrated.

l. 176. *gazette* is accented on the first syllable.

l. 191. The romantic career of Charles the Twelfth of Sweden (1682–1718) had been made familiar by Voltaire's narrative, an English translation of which was published in 1732. The explanation of Johnson's allusions may be found in any encyclopaedia, and need not be repeated here.

l. 202. *Think nothing gain'd.* Hannibal had conquered all Italy, but, says Juvenal, thought nothing accomplished, *nil actum*, till Rome should be taken. This reminds Johnson of Lucan's famous description of Caesar, who ' thought nothing done while aught remained to do '—*nil actum credens dum quid superesset agendum.*

l. 203. *Gothic*, which in the eighteenth century usually meant *Teutonic*, is here used in the specific sense of *Swedish*; cf. *Gothland*.

l. 220. *a dubious Hand* : it was suspected that Charles met his death from a chance bullet fired by his own troops.

l. 232. Johnson has altered the story ; Herodotus had been told that when his bridge across the Hellespont was destroyed, Xerxes ' commanded to give the Hellespont three hundred lashes, and to let down a pair of fetters into the sea. I have even heard that he sent branders as well, to brand the Hellespont ' (Herodotus vii. 34).

l. 241. *The bold Bavarian*: the career of Charles Albert, Elector of Bavaria, was still fresh in the public memory. In 1740, on the death of the Emperor Charles VI, he asserted his right to the imperial dominions, overran Bohemia and Austria —the 'defenceless realms' of l. 244—and was crowned Emperor in 1742. But his rival, Maria Theresa, had rallied her Hungarian subjects, and took the field against him. Other powers intervened, and Bavaria was in turn invaded. At his death in 1745 Charles Albert was a broken man.

l. 249. *Hussar* has its original sense, of Hungarian light horseman.

l. 271. *attend*: 'listen to'. This sense is illustrated, in Johnson's Dictionary, by a quotation from *The Merchant of Venice*:

> The crow doth sing as sweetly as the lark
> When neither is attended.

l. 280. *Expence*: 'extravagance'.

l. 281. *Improve*: 'augment'.

l. 291. Mrs. Piozzi in her *Anecdotes* tells us that Johnson had his mother in mind when writing these lines.

l. 313. *Lydia's Monarch*: Croesus, King of Lydia, whose wealth was fabled, entertained Solon, the wise man of Athens ; and willing to be flattered, asked Solon whom he considered to be the happiest of mortals. Solon named various persons who had died noble deaths. The King, who had expected to be told that he himself was the happiest, then asked openly if his wealth counted for nothing. The Sage replied, ' Call no man happy until he is dead '. The story is in Herodotus.

descend : from remote antiquity to the present time.

l. 317. *Marlb'rough* suffered paralysis and senile decay ; *Swift* died mad.

l. 321. *Vane*: Anne Vane, mistress of Frederick, Prince of Wales ; *Sedley*: Catharine Sedley, mistress to the Duke of York (James II).

l. 343. The conclusion of Juvenal's satire—which Macaulay judged superior in sublimity to Johnson's imitation—is thus rendered in Dryden's version :

> What then remains ? Are we depriv'd of will ?
> Must we not wish, for fear of wishing ill ?
> Receive my counsel, and securely move ;
> Intrust thy fortune to the Pow'rs above.
> Leave them to manage for thee, and to grant
> What their unerring wisdom sees thee want :
> In goodness as in greatness they excel ;
> Ah that we lov'd ourselves but half so well !
>
> *   *   *   *   *   *   *
>
> Yet not to rob the priests of pious gain,
> That altars be not wholly built in vain ;

Forgive the Gods the rest, and stand confin'd
To health of body, and content of mind :[1]
A soul, that can securely death defy,
And count it nature's privilege to die ;
Serene and manly, harden'd to sustain
The load of life, and exercis'd in pain :
Guiltless of hate, and proof against desire ;
That all things weighs, and nothing can admire :
That dares prefer the toils of Hercules
To dalliance, banquet, and ignoble ease.
   The path to peace is virtue ; what I show,
Thyself may freely on thyself bestow :
Fortune was never worshipp'd by the wise ;
But, set aloft by fools, usurps the skies.

Johnson, it will be seen, rejects the Stoic philosophy as insufficient for human happiness. ' Philosophy ', says the *Idler*, ' may infuse stubbornness, but Religion only can give Patience ' (*Idler*, No. 41).

l. 346. *darkling* is not as Johnson supposed ' a participle . . . from *darkle*, which yet I have never found ', but an adverb like *sidelong*.

On the Death of Mr. Robert Levet (p. 87).

Levet is thus described by Boswell :

' His humble friend Mr. Robert Levet, an obscure practiser in physic amongst the lower people, his fees being sometimes very small sums, sometimes whatever provisions his patients could afford him. . . . It appears from Johnson's diary, that their acquaintance commenced about the year 1746. . . . Ever since I was acquainted with Dr. Johnson, and many years before . . . , Mr. Levet had an apartment in his house, or his chambers, and waited upon him every morning, through the whole course of his late and tedious breakfast. He was of a strange, grotesque appearance, stiff and formal in his manner, and seldom said a word while any company was present.'

The Rambler (pp. 87–95).

On the merits and defects of the *Rambler* little need be added to the judgement given by Sir Walter Raleigh (pp. 54–9). But it should be noted that the current opinion of Johnson's style takes too much account of the *Rambler* and *Idler*, and neglects his maturer works, the *Journey* and the *Lives*, which are almost free from those faults of stiffness and excessive elaboration which have been found in the periodical essays. It should be noted, further, that the particular kind of

---

[1] ' Orandum est ut sit mens sana in corpore sano.'

symmetry, which, as Sir Walter Raleigh remarks, ' compels even the accidents of domestic life to happen in *contrasted pairs* ', does not seem to have disturbed Johnson's contemporaries, who were more accustomed than we are to that manner of writing. The faults upon which his detractors and parodists fastened were, firstly, the abuse of Latin polysyllables, secondly, the trick of what they called *triplets* or *triads*. Most of the contemporary parodies are so exaggerated as to be scarcely amusing ; the most notorious of these is the anonymous *Lexiphanes, A Dialogue, imitated from Lucian, and suited to the present times ; being an attempt to restore the English Tongue to its ancient purity, and to correct, as well as expose, the affected Style, hard Words, and absurd Phraseology of many late Writers, and particularly of our English Lexiphanes, the Rambler*. The following sentences, chosen from this book, attempt to ridicule both these mannerisms : ' Eubulus, though he could hardly articulate for a suffocation of risibility, declared with profound sacramental obtestation, that he had himself laboured under similar powers of deception. I believed him not, and threatened to convict him of the tortuosity of his imaginary rectitude by manual syllogisms, fistical applications, and baculinary argumentation.'

PAGE **91,** l. 7. *philosophy* means what is now called natural science. (In some Universities the Professor of Physics is still called Professor of Natural Philosophy.) On the other hand, *science* at one time could mean what we commonly call philosophy.

l. 17. *at Chelsea* : in the *Physick Garden* there.

PAGE **94,** l. 17. *Atalanta* stopped to pick up golden apples, dropped by her crafty competitor, and so lost the race.

The Dictionary (pp. 96–102).

Johnson published his *Plan* in 1747 ; and in 1755 appeared *A Dictionary of the English Language, in which the Words are deduced from their Original, and illustrated in their different Significations by Examples from the Best Writers*. The common English dictionary until Johnson's time, and indeed long afterwards, was that of Nathaniel Bailey. But Bailey's book was a mere vocabulary with etymologies ; Johnson may be said to have founded modern English lexicography, by his discrimination of the senses of words and by his illustrative quotations. ' Johnson's great work ', wrote Sir James Murray, the first editor of the Oxford Dictionary, ' raised English lexicography to a higher level. In his hands it became a department of literature.'

Johnson in this ambitious undertaking attempted to rival the Dictionaries of the *Académie française* and the Italian

Accademia della Crusca ; his book, like theirs, embodied an attempt to *ascertain* the language, which it was supposed had become settled, and might be preserved from decay by proscribing innovations and irregularities. Johnson was aware that this attempt could not wholly succeed (see p. 100) ; we now know that it was doomed to failure. He cannot, however, be accused of taking a narrow view, or of attempting to confine the literary vocabulary to the usage of his own time. He was, on the contrary, careful to preserve the treasures of a former age, and to enrich the language by drawing from *the wells of English undefiled*, the diction of the Bible and of Shakespeare.

Johnson's method of compilation was to mark passages in the books which he read for the purpose. These were transcribed by his amanuenses. A reader who turns the pages of the Dictionary soon discovers that Johnson's reading for it, though wide, was limited to such authors as he judged sufficient for his purpose. Shakespeare, Spenser, Milton, Dryden, Pope, Bacon, Hooker, appear again and again on every page. It is obvious that one man, attempting such a task, must limit himself in this way ; the inference drawn by Macaulay (see p. 32), that he was ignorant of the minor Elizabethan dramatists, because he does not quote them in his Dictionary, is not legitimate. Further, ' Johnson's *Dictionary* was intended primarily to furnish a standard of polite usage, suitable for the classic ideals of the new age. He was therefore obliged to forgo the use of the lesser Elizabethans, whose authority no one acknowledged, and whose freedom and extravagance were enemies to his purpose ' (Sir Walter Raleigh, in *Johnson on Shakespeare*).

PAGE **96.** For Johnson's relations with Lord Chesterfield see the famous Letter (p. 159, and note on p. 193).

PAGE **98,** l. 24. *a favourite name* : David Garrick is quoted under *giggle*, Charlotte Lennox's *Female Quixote* under *talent*.

l. 28. *wells of English undefiled* : *Faerie Queene*, IV. ii. 32. Dan Chaucer, well of English undefyled.

l. 32. *Gallick structure*. Elsewhere he speaks of the danger that Englishmen may be ' reduced to babble a dialect of *France* ' ; and he declared that Hume's prose was French in structure. The perils of a French invasion were much talked of, then and later ; the fashionable periodical called *The World* condemned words imported from the French, or altered in meaning by French influence. Many years later, Miss Burney, in *Cecilia*, parodied the fashion of Gallicism in the person of a young man who introduces French words into every sentence. Very little damage was done, in the end, to the English language, which has always been tolerant of foreign visitors ; but the danger was no doubt real. The best judges agree that the ' *Gallick* structure ' is traceable in Hume, and also in Gibbon.

PAGE **99,** l. 32. *Original* : we now say *origin* ; cf. Dryden's *Original and Progress of Satire.* The plan which Johnson abandoned has been pursued by many modern compilers, who have made a *Dictionary* serve also the uses of an *Encyclopaedia.*

PAGE **100,** l. 35. *risible absurdities* : when a lady asked Johnson why he defined *pastern* as *the knee of a horse,* she expected a sophistical defence ; to her astonishment he replied, ' Ignorance, Madam ; pure ignorance '.

PAGE **101,** l. 9. *a whole life would not be sufficient.* The Oxford Dictionary, which aims at finality, is still incomplete, after nearly forty years of continuous production by a large number of workers.

PAGE **102,** l. 11. *those whom I wished to please.* The Dictionary, planned in 1747, was published in 1755. Johnson's wife died in 1752.

The Idler (pp. 103–10).

What has been said of the *Rambler* may be applied without alteration to the *Idler.* The only important difference noted by contemporaries was that the *Idler* had a somewhat lighter touch.

The paper on *Tom Tempest* and *Jack Sneaker* shows Johnson's play of humour at its best. It is not equal to Addison, but does not fall far short of its model.

The Life and Opinions of *Dick Minim* may be called an introduction to the history of Taste in his day. It cannot, of course, be fully enjoyed without more knowledge of the subject than can be communicated in brief notes. It would have been wiser, perhaps, to leave it without comment. But in turning the leaves of the *Lives of the Poets,* in search of confirmation or confutation of Minim's critical dicta, I found so many delightful sentences that I could not forgo the pleasure of quoting a few of them.

PAGE **103,** ll. 16–20. *Cartesian* : a follower of René Descartes, who has been called the founder of modern philosophy. *Malbranche,* or Malebranche, a French Cartesian.

Berkeley : George Berkeley, Bishop of Cloyne in Ireland. Johnson's description of the doctrines of these philosophers is that of an unsympathetic ' plain man '. Descartes was what is called a *dualist,* believing that Mind and Matter are opposite and independent. Malebranche was a Pantheist, who ' saw everything in God ' ; we know things as a part of God's knowledge of them, imparted by him to us. Berkeley denied any real existence whatever to Material Substance ; nothing **is real** except God and ' spirits ' ; man is a spirit, and his sensations are real, but are not sensations *of* anything real that is outside him.

PAGE **104,** l. 32. *Tillotson* : John Tillotson, first Archbishop of Canterbury under William and Mary ; a famous preacher.

l. 33. *owns that she meant well* : Anne was suspected of conniving at attempts to restore the Pretender, James Edward.

PAGE **105,** l. 3. *Dettingen* : in 1743 George II in person led his army to victory against the French at Dettingen ; in 1745 the British, under the Duke of Cumberland, and their allies, were beaten by the French, under Marshal Saxe, at Fontenoy.

ll. 4–6. I learn from the *Gentleman's Magazine* that the *Victory* was wrecked off Alderney in 1744 ; that the Cornhill fire broke out in Mr. Eldridge's, a peruke-maker in Exchange Alley, on 25 March 1748, and burned down eighty houses ; and that the sinking of the piers of Westminster Bridge (begun 1738) was likened by political satirists to Sir Robert Walpole's *sinking fund.*

l. 21. *conveyed in a warming-pan* : James Edward, the son of James II by his Roman Catholic Queen, was born in 1688, just before the flight of his parents. Interested politicians put about the story that he was not the Queen's child.

l. 27. *the peace of Utrecht,* 1713, brought to an end the War of the Spanish Succession, in which Marlborough won his famous victories over the French generals. By its terms Louis XIV recognized the Protestant Succession in Great Britain, and abandoned the project of uniting France and Spain under one dynasty.

l. 34. *the electoral dominions* : of Hanover. George I and George II were always ready to sacrifice the interests of England to those of their Hanoverian dominions.

PAGE **106,** l. 14. *Criticism.* ' Who are the critics ? ' asks the great artist in *Lothair* ; ' those who have failed in literature and art.'

PAGE **107,** l. 2. *No genius was ever blasted* : ' No man ', said Bentley, ' was ever written down but by himself.' Johnson was fond of quoting this.

l. 29. *a few select writers.* Mr. Nichol Smith points out to me that Minim's solitude need not have been very laborious ; all that he brought back from Richmond may be found in the Works of Pope. See the *Essay on Criticism* (l. 68, ' First follow Nature ' ; l. 82, ' wit and judgment often are at strife '), the *Epistle to Augustus* (l. 281, ' the last and greatest Art, the Art to blot '), and the *Epistle to Dr. Arbuthnot* (l. 40, ' this saving counsel, " Keep your piece nine years ".').

PAGE **108,** l. 9. The censure of Spenser is Dryden's, who in *The Original and Progress of Satire* speaks of ' the ill choice of his stanza ', though allowing that ' he is the more to be admired, that, labouring under such a difficulty, his verses are so numerous (i.e. *rhythmical*), so various, and so harmonious, that only Virgil . . . has surpassed him among the Romans ; and only Mr. Waller among the English '. Johnson himself (*Rambler*, 121) thought the Spenserian stanza ' at once difficult and tiresome ; tiresome to the ear by its uniformity, and to the attention by its length '.

the hexameters of Sidney. Cf. Pope, *Epistle to Augustus*, l. 98, ' And Sidney's verse halts ill on Roman feet'.

l. 10.   *Denham and Waller.* Minim's dicta may be illustrated from the *Lives of the Poets*. Of Denham, the author of *Cooper's Hill*, Johnson says that he ' is deservedly considered as one of the fathers of English poetry ' ; and he quotes the judgement of Prior, that ' Denham and Waller improved our versification, and Dryden perfected it '. ' The strength of Denham ' was Pope's phrase (*Essay on Criticism*, l. 361).   His style may be illustrated by four lines from *Cooper's Hill*, which were praised by Dryden, and became famous :

> O could I flow like thee, and make thy stream
> My great example, as it is my theme !
> Though deep, yet clear ; though gentle, yet not dull ;
> Strong without rage, without o'erflowing full.

In the *Life of Waller* Johnson says : ' He was rather smooth than strong ; of *the full resounding line*, which Pope attributes to Dryden, he has given very few examples.   The critical decision has given the praise of strength to Denham, and of sweetness to Waller.'

Waller is best remembered as a writer of occasional verses. A good specimen of his lighter manner is this compliment to a lady :

> Some other nymphs, with colours faint,
> And pencil slow, may Cupid paint,
> And a weak heart in time destroy ;
> She has a stamp, and prints the Boy.

l. 17.   *All for Love, or the World Well Lost* (1678), Dryden's best play.   It deals with the story of Antony and Cleopatra, and owes much to Shakespeare's play.   In it he forsook rhyme, for the use of which in tragedy he had fought hard (see p. 144, l. 9, and note).   He says in his preface : ' In my style, I have professed to imitate the divine Shakespeare ; which that I might perform more freely, I have disencumbered myself from rhyme.   Not that I condemn my former way, but that this is more proper to my present purpose.'

The opening scene, between Antony and Ventidius, was preferred by Dryden himself ' to anything which I have written in this kind '.   The first speech may be quoted :

> *Antony.* They tell me 'tis my birthday, and I'll keep it
> With double pomp of sadness.

'Tis what the day deserves that gave me breath.
Why was I raised the meteor of the world
Hung in the skies, and blazing as I travelled
Till all my fires are spent ; and then cast downward
To be trod out by Caesar ?

l. 20. *Otway* : Thomas Otway's tragedy, *Venice Preserved,
A Plot Discover'd* (1682), founded on a French account of the
Spanish Plot against Venice in 1618, held the stage for more
than a century. ' The striking passages ', writes Johnson in
the *Life of Otway*, ' are in every mouth ; and the publick
seems to judge rightly of the faults and excellences of this
play, that it is the work of a man not attentive to decency,
nor zealous for virtue ; but of one who conceived forcibly,
and drew originally, by consulting nature in his own
breast.'

l. 24. *Southern* : His *Fatal Marriage* (1694) was very
successful in its day, and was revived by Garrick a year or
two before the date of the *Idler*.

l. 28. *Rowe* : Nicholas Rowe, dramatist, translator, and the
first editor of Shakespeare. His *Fair Penitent* (1703), which
Johnson thought ' one of the most pleasing tragedies on the
stage ', is best remembered for the name of Lothario, the
prototype of Richardson's Lovelace. ' Lothario, with gaiety
which cannot be hated, and bravery which cannot be despised,
retains too much of the spectator's kindness.' Rowe's translation of the *Pharsalia* of Lucan Johnson pronounced to be
' one of the greatest productions of English poetry ; for there
is perhaps none that so completely exhibits the genius and
spirit of the original '.

l. 30. *Congreve* : ' his characters are commonly fictitious
and artificial, with very little of nature, and not much of
life . . . his personages are a kind of intellectual gladiators ;
every sentence is to ward or strike ; the contest of smart-
ness is never intermitted ' (*Life of Congreve*).

l. 32. *Cato* : see p. 125, and note (p. 187).

l. 34. *as a critick* : ' His criticism is condemned as tentative
or experimental, rather than scientifick, and he is considered
as deciding by taste rather than by principles.' But Johnson
did not subscribe to the common opinion : ' Before the
profound observers of the present race repose too securely
in the consciousness of their superiority to Addison, let them
consider his *Remarks on Ovid*, in which may be found specimens of criticism sufficiently subtle and refined ; let them
peruse likewise his essays on *Wit*, and on the *Pleasures of
Imagination*, in which he founds art on the base of nature,
and draws the principles of invention from dispositions

inherent in the mind of man, with skill and elegance, such as his contemners will not easily attain.'

l. 35. *Prior*, writes Johnson, ' has tried all styles, from the grotesque to the solemn, and has not so failed in any as to incur derision or disgrace '. His *Tales* are ' written with great familiarity and great spriteliness '. His *Solomon* was the occasion of this memorable judgement : ' Tediousness is the most fatal of all faults ; negligence or errors are single and local, but tediousness pervades the whole ; other faults are censured and forgotten, but the power of tediousness propagates itself. He that is weary the first hour, is more weary the second.'

PAGE **109,** l. 6. *rather luscious than sweet* : ' His poetry has been censured as too uniformly musical, and as glutting the ear with unvaried sweetness. I suspect this objection to be the cant of those who judge by principles rather than perception ' (*Life of Pope*).

l. 7. *Phaedra and Hippolitus* : a blank verse tragedy (1708) by Edmund Smith. Minim got his opinion from Addison : ' Would one think it was possible (at a time when an author lived that was able to write the *Phaedra and Hippolitus*) for a people to be so stupidly fond of the Italian opera as scarce to give a third day's hearing to that admirable tragedy ? ' (*Spectator*, No. 18). Johnson, in the *Life of Smith*, says, ' His play pleased the criticks, and the criticks only '. Yet it is printed in full, beside *Cato*, in the *Elegant Extracts*.

l. 24. *love predominates*. For Johnson's own view on this question see p. 122.

PAGE **110,** l. 1. *Barbarossa* : a tragedy by John Brown (1755).

l. 2. *Cleone* : a tragedy by Robert Dodsley the bookseller, better known as the producer of *A Collection of Poems by Several Hands* (always known as ' Dodsley's Collection ') and a *Select Collection of Old Plays*. *Cleone* was played at Covent Garden in December 1758, six months before this *Idler* was written.

The Prince of Abissinia (pp. 111–19).

The story of the composition of *Rasselas* may be read in Boswell. ' This admirable performance, which, though he had written nothing else, would have rendered his name immortal in the world of literature,' was written, we are informed, in the evenings of a single week ; and twenty years later Johnson said ' he had not looked at it since it was first published '. Here Johnson's memory failed him, for he had corrected it for a later edition ; it is clear, however, that he did not regard it as one of his greatest works. The extravagant praise of Boswell and others has reacted unfavourably on modern readers, whose expectations have been pitched too high. Those who look for a compendium of human philosophy will be disappointed in *Rasselas* ; but if it is read for what it professes to be, a *Moral Tale*, it will be found full of kindly humour, and of a placid solemnity which may sometimes be risible, but is always lovable.

The scene of the *Dissertation on the Art of Flying* is the Happy Valley in which the Abyssinian princes and princesses are confined, with every luxury except freedom to pass the mountain barrier. In the next chapter we find that Rasselas, with the Princess Nekayah and her attendant Pekuah, have escaped with the philosophic Imlac, and are mixing in the world under his guidance.

PAGE **115,** l. 17. *When the claims of the publick were satisfied.* ' A man is to have part of his life to himself,' Johnson once said.

Johnson on Shakespeare (pp. 120–8).

Johnson projected an edition of Shakespeare as early as 1745, but his first Proposals were abortive. When the Dictionary had established his fame, he returned to his former design, and published in 1756 *Proposals for Printing the Dramatick Works of William Shakespeare*. In 1762, when the work was still far from completion, his pension set him free from drudgery ; and it began to seem as if his subscribers might never get their Shakespeare. More good stories are told about this than we have space to quote. To a bookseller who brought a subscription, and modestly asked that the subscriber's name might be printed according to custom, ' I shall print no list of subscribers ', said Johnson, with great abruptness : then, more complacently, ' Sir, I have two very urgent reasons for not printing any list of subscribers ;—one, that I have lost all the names,—the other, that I have spent all the money '. Churchill in *The Ghost*, published in 1762, accused *Pomposo* of breach of faith :

> He for subscribers baits his hook,
> And takes their cash ; but where's the book ?

We do not know that this had any more terrors for Johnson than a hundred other squibs ; but he was somehow persuaded to make an end ; and the edition in eight volumes appeared at last in 1765.

All, and much more than all, that may fairly be said in depreciation of Johnson's work as an editor, may be read in Macaulay's *Life* (pp. 30–2). The contrary view, which has gained ground, is indicated by Sir Walter Raleigh in his *Essay* (p. 72), and stated at length elsewhere by the same writer (see his *Johnson on Shakespeare*, the Introduction to which is reprinted in his *Six Essays on Johnson*).

The passages chosen from the *Preface* sufficiently illustrate Johnson's admiration for the *transcendent and unbounded genius* of Shakespeare. There is no justification for regarding him as a detractor from Shakespeare's fame. It is true that Johnson shared to some extent the notions of his age about Shakespeare's laxities and irregularities, his want of what was called correctness ; notions from which modern critics dissent. We feel that in comparing so poor a thing as *Cato* with *Othello*—though the comparison is to Addison's disadvantage—Johnson shows some lack of perspective. But the common belief that Johnson was blind to the real greatness of Shakespeare rests on a misconception. Johnson is not voicing a general insensibility, but sets out to save Shakespeare from the excessive and indiscriminate adulation of Garrick and his school, who, as he said, ' know not how to blame, nor how to commend '. 'Johnson,' says Boswell, ' by candidly admitting the faults of his poet, had the more credit in bestowing on him deserved and indisputable praise ; and doubtless none of all his panegyrists have done him half so much honour.'

In his discussion of Shakespeare's faults, which, then and since, has offended the susceptibilities of many, Johnson was only claiming the privilege of a critic to treat his author as a man and a poet, and not as the object of an unreasoning idolatry. That Shakespeare has the faults with which Johnson charges him—faults of negligence, or of excessive indulgence in verbal gymnastics—can be denied only by those who, when they read Shakespeare, resign the exercise of all critical discernment.

PAGE **120,** l. 2. *revision* now implies alteration ; Johnson writes *revise* where we should write *edit*. Thus he says of *King Lear* that ' I was many years ago so shocked by *Cordelia's* death, that I know not whether I ever endured to read again the last scenes of the play till I undertook to revise them as an editor '.

PAGE **121,** l. 24. *individual . . . species*. If a modern critic said of a dramatist that his characters are rather types than individuals, he would intend not praise but blame. The context shows that this is not Johnson's meaning. He does not mean that Shakespeare's characters are what we should call generalized types, but that they exhibit the qualities common to humanity ; that they speak and act like men and women ; and he seems to contrast them with the creations of inferior playwrights, who seek to make their puppets lifelike by labelling them with tricks and mannerisms.

l. 35. *Hierocles* : the author of a Greek collection of jokes. Johnson was no doubt familiar with *Beauties of Shakespeare,* published in 1752. The compiler was Dr. William Dodd, who (as anthologists may do well to remember) was afterwards hanged for forgery.

PAGE **123,** l. 7. *Pope* : in the Preface to his edition of Shakespeare : ' To this life and variety of Character, we must add the wonderful preservation of it ; which is such throughout his Plays, that had all the Speeches been printed without the very names of the Persons, I believe one might have apply'd them with certainty to every speaker.'

PAGE **125,** l. 11. *Cato.* Little is now remembered of this once famous play except the familiar

> 'Tis not in mortals to command success,
> But we'll do more, Sempronius, we'll deserve it.

It would not be easy to select from *Cato* any single passage that should be more, or less, representative of the whole than any other ; it is throughout dignified, smooth, and frigid. A few lines may be quoted from Cato's soliloquy in the last act. The philosopher patriot holds in one hand the sword with which he will take his life, in the other ' Plato's book on the Immortality of the Soul ' :

> Thus am I doubly arm'd : my death and life,
> My bane and antidote are both before me.
> This in a moment brings me to an end ;
> But this informs me I shall never die.
> The soul, secur'd in her existence, smiles
> At the drawn dagger, and defies its point.
> The stars shall fade away, the sun himself
> Grow dim with age, and nature sink in years,
> But thou shalt flourish in immortal youth,
> Unhurt amidst the war of elements,
> The wreck of matter, and the crush of worlds.

Convention permitted, in a blank verse tragedy, a few rhyming lines at the end of an act (see p. 110 for Dick Minim's condemnation of this licence). It is interesting to note that these lines are the best, because the least unnatural, in the play. The last Act ends thus :

> From hence, let fierce contending nations know
> What dire effects from civil discord flow.
> 'Tis this that shakes our country with alarms,
> And gives up Rome a prey to Roman arms,
> Produces fraud, and cruelty, and strife,
> And robs the guilty world of Cato's life.

Falkland's Islands (pp. 129–30).

Falkland's Islands is one of four political tracts written by Johnson between 1770 and 1775, in the interest, and doubtless at the request, of Government. They were hurriedly composed, and show too much of the spirit of party ; and they did not add to Johnson's reputation. But they contain some memorable passages.

It is impossible to read this description of the miseries and losses consequent upon a protracted war, without being struck by the closeness of its application to our own experience. In one point, indeed, and that the most important of all, the wars of the eighteenth century, and even the ' Great ' Napoleonic war, differed from the late catastrophe ; for only a fraction of the nation had any part in them. That is why it was possible for Johnson to urge his paradox, that ' public affairs vex no man ' ; that is why the novels of his day, like those of Jane Austen, are full of young men doing nothing in particular, and doing it without reproach.

But everything else is here : the thoughtless popular confidence in a speedy victory ; the long misery of the campaign, with its necessary and its unnecessary hardship, disease, and death ; the growing burden of taxation ; and finally the ' sudden glories ' of those whom we call ' profiteers '.

PAGE **129,** l. 1. *cuncta prius tentanda* : everything else must first be tried.

A Journey to the Western Islands (pp. 131–6).

Johnson declared that ' when a man is tired of London, he is tired of Life ' ; but he was fond of excursions into the rural wilderness, and in particular had long desired to visit the Western Islands, where he might see a state of society which in England had long since passed away. The pertinacity of Boswell brought this wish to realization ; Johnson joined him in Edinburgh in August, 1773. They drove in a post-chaise as far as Inverness, rode to the west coast on hired horses, and crossed to Skye. Thereafter they travelled among the Islands as they could, in boats or on the backs of rough ponies, in weather typical of the Hebridean summer, for it rained almost continuously.

This adventure produced two notable books ; Johnson's *Journey* and Boswell's *Journal of a Tour to the Hebrides with Samuel Johnson, LL.D.*, which formed the first instalment of the Life of Johnson. It was written, for the most part, at the time or soon afterwards, and was read by Johnson and others in manuscript. It was published in 1785, soon after Johnson's death ; its great success encouraged Boswell to carry on his work.

PAGE **131,** l. 1. *this uniformity of barrenness.* Johnson shared the view, common in his time, that mountains are merely ' horrid ', and tracts of heather merely melancholy. Of the marvellous panorama of the Islands, transfigured by the soft

Atlantic sunshine, he probably saw very little. But he was not always insensible of the beauty of the scene, as this extract shows ; see also p. 136.

l. 19. *a narrow valley* : Glen Sheil. From the glen their way lay over Mam Rattachen, by General Wade's zigzag road, and down to Glenelg, where they took boat for Skye.

PAGE **135,** l. 24. The travellers visited Inchkenneth, where they were the guests of Sir Allan Maclean, who conducted them to Icolmkill (' Columba's island '), better known as Iona.

PAGE **136,** l. 10. *the fault which I have just been censuring* : they had visited a cave, and Johnson blames himself for being ' unprovided with instruments for taking heights and distances '.

l. 20. *We were now treading* : this famous piece owes much of its melody to those classical cadences which lend beauty to the *Book of Common Prayer,* and to all the rhythmical or ' numerous ' prose of the seventeenth century. The classical *laws* persisted into the Middle Ages, and the tradition was never lost. According to the rule a sentence should end with an *accented syllable* followed by *two or three unaccented syllables,* which combination is itself followed by a *trochaic or dactylic cadence* ; $-\cup\cup$ or $-\cup\cup\cup$ followed by $-\cup$ or $-\cup\cup$ or $-\cup-\cup$. Thus : il*lustrious island,* Cale*donian region* $(-\cup\cup/-\cup)$; *roving barbarians* $(-\cup\cup/$ $-\cup\cup)$; *ruins of Iona* $(-\cup\cup\cup/-\cup)$; *dignity of thinking beings* $(-\cup\cup\cup/-\cup-\cup)$. See also p. 156, the *Dedication to the King.*

The Lives of the Poets (pp. 137–49).

The story of this fortunate undertaking is told by Boswell ; see Macaulay's *Life,* pp. 43–5, and Raleigh's *Essay,* pp. 67–70. The *Lives* are an indispensable introduction to the history of English poetry from Cowley to Gray, and one of the most entertaining books in the world.

Johnson's intention was to write mere prefaces ; but he was, as he writes in the *Advertisement,* ' led beyond my intention, I hope, by the honest desire of giving useful pleasure '. These *Lives* and the *Journey* were the only books which Johnson wrote to please himself.

The *Prefaces,* afterwards called *Lives,* first appeared as volumes 1–10 of the collection, for which, though it was often labelled *Johnson's Poets,* Johnson had no responsibility. It was originally intended to begin with Chaucer, and we do not know why the design was altered.

PAGE **137,** l. 1. *Addison* : *Spectator,* No. 273, ' the principal Actors in this Poem are not only our Progenitors, but our Representatives. We have an actual Interest in everything they do, and no less than our utmost Happiness is concerned, and lies at Stake in all their Behaviour.'

l. 8. *heroic* : the same as *epic* ; *epic* is from *epos*, the *Word,
Saga* ; *heroic* poetry was so called because it celebrated the deeds
of the *Heroes* or demi-gods, sons of a god and a mortal mother,
as Hercules, or of a goddess and a mortal father, as Achilles.
The dactylic hexameter of the Homeric poems was called by
the Greeks the *heroic rhythm.*

l. 12. *Dryden* : in the *Dedication of the Æneis* : ' if the Devil
had not been his hero, instead of Adam ; if the giant had not
foiled the knight, and driven him out of his stronghold, to
wander through the world with his lady errant.'

l. 15. *established practice* : Johnson would not admit the
doctrine of what is called *poetical justice.*

PAGE **138,** l. 8. *that fortitude* : *Paradise Lost,* v. 898 :

> Among innumerable false, unmov'd,
> Unshak'n, unseduc'd, unterrifi'd
> His Loyaltie he kept, his Love, his Zeale ;
> Nor number, nor example with him wrought
> To swerve from truth, or change his constant mind
> Though single.

l. 11. *Raphael's reproof* : *Paradise Lost,* viii ; the tenor of
Raphael's speech is shown in (167) :

> Sollicit not thy thoughts with matters hid,
> Leave them to God above, him serve and feare.

And that of Adam's reply in :

> to know
> That which before us lies in daily life,
> Is the prime Wisdom, what is more, is fume,
> Is emptiness, or fond impertinence.

PAGE **139,** l. 15. *Criticism.* Johnson explains that Dryden's
plays brought him profit from three sources : the benefit
night, the dedication (paid for by the patron), and the ' copy ',
or, as we say, copyright, which he sold to a bookseller.   ' To
increase the value of his copies, he often accompanied his
work with a preface of criticism ; a kind of learning then
almost new in the English language.'   The most famous of
the critical works is the *Essay of Dramatic Poesy.*   Johnson
thought so highly of Dryden's prose, as to conclude his own
Preface to Shakespeare with the great passage which begins :

' Shakespeare was the man, who, of all modern and perhaps
ancient poets, had the largest and most comprehensive soul.'

PAGE **140,** l. 2. *another and the same* : *alter et idem;*
' another, yet the same ', in Pope's *Dunciad.*

l. 14. *as* means *in proportion as.*   The modern use or
misuse, which makes *as*, in such a sentence as this, merely
causal in force, was unknown to Johnson.

l. 17. *Absalom and Achitophel* : published in 1681, and

directed against the attempt of Shaftesbury and his party to exclude the Duke of York from the succession as a papist, and to secure it for Charles II's natural son, the Duke of Monmouth (Absalom).

PAGE 141, l. 13. *the king makes a speech* :

> He said : Th' Almighty nodding gave consent ;
> And peals of thunder shook the firmament.
> Henceforth a series of new time began,
> The mighty years in long procession ran :
> Once more the god-like David was restor'd,
> And willing nations knew their lawful lord.

There is, of course, nothing in the speech to account for this sudden dissipation of the terrors raised by the poem, which therefore comes to an absurd end.

l. 19. I have added this passage—reluctantly truncated—as a supplement to the rest. It shows that we do wrong to think—as many are tempted to think—that the poets and critics of Dryden's time, and of Johnson's, knew nothing of the half lights, the meanings which haunt and elude, in which we now find such magic. It is true that Johnson censures some of the lines he here quotes ; but is it not an indulgent censure ? Dryden had confessed that some lines in his plays were bad ; ' but I knew that they were bad enough to please, even when I wrote them '. Johnson's comment is this : ' There is surely reason enough to suspect that he pleased himself as well as his audience.' This is shrewd criticism ; but it is not the language of disgust ; we may be sure that the critic, like the poet, had a relish for ' treading upon the brink of meaning '.

PAGE 142, l. 26. *sapere et fari* : from *sapere* is derived *sapientia, wisdom ; fari* is to speak articulately, of intelligible human speech as distinguished from the babbling of *in-fantes.*

l. 27. *Davis* : Sir John Davies, a younger contemporary of Shakespeare. He wrote a poem, *Nosce Teipsum* (' Know Thyself '), on the immortality of the soul. It is written in quatrains, of the same form as *Annus Mirabilis.*

l. 33. *he left it marble.* It is tempting to linger over the *Life of Dryden*, which of all the *Lives* is written with the greatest zest. The most generous of men and critics, Johnson never conceals his dislikes ; and, political prejudices apart, it seems that both Milton and Addison were characters uncongenial to him ; that he found Milton too much a pedant, and Addison too much a calculator. It is certain that he was repelled by the misanthropy of Swift, the artifice of Pope, and the foppery of Gray. But in the life of Dryden there was nothing for Johnson to dislike. He might find some want of principle in his behaviour, and great want of decency in his works; but such vices did not alienate Johnson's sympathy. There was much in Dryden to excite it; like himself he was a professional writer, who wrote for money and in haste; he resembled him, too, in his masculine judgement, his keen-edged wit, his immense fertility. The result is that the *Life of Dryden* exhibits both its subject and its author in the most amiable light. Johnson rejoices in Dryden's strength, and in his own.

PAGE **143.** *Edmund Smith.* This extract has no reference to Smith, the forgotten author of *Phaedra and Hippolitus* (see p. 109 and note). Dr Gilbert Walmesley, Registrar of the Ecclesiastical Court of Lichfield, befriended Johnson in his youth, invited him to his house, and gave him introductions when he went to London. Johnson never forgot a friend, and his earliest friends were those he loved best.

l. 30. *David Garrick* died in 1779. *Eclipsed the gaiety of nations*: Boswell ventured to suggest that the expression was hyperbolical. JOHNSON: 'I could not have said more or less. It is the truth, *eclipsed*, not *extinguished*; and his death *did* eclipse; it was like a storm.' Cf. *Adonais*:

> The splendours of the firmament of time
> May be eclipsed, but are extinguished not.

PAGE **144,** l. 9. *poetical prejudices*: of these the chief was his love for rhyme, the use of which he vigorously defended in *Of Dramatick Poesie, an Essay* (1668), and by his own practice. But he gave it up when he wrote *All for Love* in imitation of Shakespeare. See note on p. 108, l. 17 (p. 182).

l. 10. *unnatural thoughts and rugged numbers*: the harsh metres, and extravagances of thought and language, found especially in Donne and his imitators. Johnson in the *Life of Dryden* writes: 'Dryden very early formed his versification: there are in this early production [a poem published in 1658] no traces of Donne's or Jonson's ruggedness; but he did not so soon free his mind from the ambition of forced conceits.'

PAGE **145,** l. 2. *Thirty-eight*: *One Thousand Seven Hundred and Thirty-eight, a Dialogue something like Horace*; published on the same day (1738) as *London, a Poem*.

PAGE **147,** l. 7. *Warburton*: William Warburton, Bishop of Gloucester, a man of great learning and ingenuity; indeed of excessive ingenuity, for Johnson said (of his notes on Shakespeare) that he had 'a rage for saying something when there is nothing to be said'. He was Pope's literary executor, and edited the collected works published in 1751.

The Bravery of the English Common Soldiers (pp. 153–5).

This remarkable piece is one of the *Additional Essays* printed in the third edition of the *Idler*. There is no better example of the power and originality of Johnson's thought on political subjects. The relevance of this essay to some political problems of to-day is even startling; we are not accustomed to read political reflections, written a century and a half ago, and to find in them a searching analysis of our own society.

PAGE **153**, l. 6. *sentences*. *Sentence* is the Latin *sententia*, *thought*, and in Johnson's time meant properly a maxim or opinion—not, as now, any number of words forming a grammatical whole.

l. 15. *clowns*. *Clown* is defined by Johnson as ' a rustick ' ; *boor* is used in the same sense.

Dedications (pp. 156–7).

' In that courtly species of composition ', writes Boswell, ' no man excelled Dr. Johnson. Though the loftiness of his mind prevented him from ever dedicating in his own person, he wrote a very great number of Dedications for others. . . . He told me . . . " he believed he had dedicated to all the Royal Family round ". . . . He once dedicated some Musick for the German Flute to Edward, Duke of York.'

The specimens given are fine examples of Johnson's most ornate style. For their rhythmical cadences see the note on p. 136. The first paragraph on p. 157 is an example of the kind of inversion which Milton and his contemporaries copied from their Latin models, and which Johnson was almost the last to practise.

Letter to Lord Chesterfield (pp. 158–60).

Boswell tells us, on Dodsley's authority, that Lord Chesterfield let the letter lie upon his table, where anybody might see it ; he even read it to Dodsley, ' pointed out the severest passages, and observed how well they were expressed '.

Boswell published the letter separately in 1790, in a half-guinea quarto, with notes.

PAGE **160**, l. 17. *The shepherd in Virgil : Eclogues*, viii. 43, ' I know thee, Love ! in deserts thou wast hid ' (Dryden's translation).

Letter to James Macpherson (pp. 161–2).

Macpherson published in Edinburgh in 1760 *Fragments of Ancient Poetry collected in the Highlands of Scotland*, and, encouraged by success, produced in London in 1762 *Fingal, an ancient epic poem*. A fierce controversy raged over the ' poems of Ossian ' ; most Englishmen, following Johnson, denounced them as forgeries ; most Scotsmen, including Blair, ' conspired ' to proclaim them genuine. It is a pathetic story. Macpherson, who at first had perhaps hardly hoped to deceive, was at last obliged to satisfy his supporters by producing the poems he professed to translate ; subscriptions were raised to pay for their publication, and he sat down to forge ' originals ' in a language with which he was very imperfectly acquainted. The real merits of his *Ossian*, which are great, were largely obscured by his false pretensions.

Johnson's letter is extant, in the collection of Mr. R. B. Adam of Buffalo, and differs a good deal from the version dictated from memory ; but the differences are only verbal.

Private Letters (pp. 163–8).

Johnson's letters were eagerly collected after his death, and many of them were published in the magazines. The first collection was Mrs. Piozzi's *Letters to and from the late Samuel Johnson* (1788). Boswell printed all he could find *except* those published by Mrs. Piozzi; and more were added by Malone, and later by Croker, in successive editions of Boswell's *Life*. Finally, Dr. Birkbeck Hill in 1892 produced an edition of all the letters known to him (except those included in his own edition of Boswell's *Life*).

But Johnson has never been one of the popular letter-writers, like Walpole or Cowper. The familiar letters to Mrs. Thrale show a side of him to which Boswell was not in a position to do complete justice ; they have what Fanny Burney thought their writer had, ' more fun, and comical humour, and love of nonsense, than almost any body I ever saw '. But the other letters have a characteristic austerity, and for that reason are not much relished except by those who have learned to enjoy also what Johnson wrote for the press. Yet they are full of wisdom, and they have more tenderness than Johnson often allowed to appear in anything he published.

PAGE **163**. *To George Strahan*. This was the son of Johnson's friend William Strahan, the printer. He was a clergyman, and edited Johnson's *Prayers and Meditations*.

PAGE **164**, l. 16. *To Mrs. Thrale*. See Macaulay's account of Johnson's long association with Mrs. Thrale ; his romantic affection for her is proved by the letters, some hundreds of which have survived. When her husband died, in 1781, she grew weary of Johnson. Boswell says that ' as her vanity had been fully gratified, by having the Colossus of Literature attached to her for many years, she gradually became less assiduous to please him '. Mrs. Thrale herself pleads that in spite of her ' veneration for his virtue, reverence for his talents, and delight in his conversation ', she found herself unable, after her husband's death, to bear the burden of constant attendance. We may believe that Johnson was exacting, the more so as he grew old and ill. But Mrs. Thrale's discovery was convenient ; for she wanted to do what she knew would end the connexion. This was to marry ' Signor Piozzi, an Italian musick-master '. Most people now think that she had a perfect right to please herself in marrying the man she loved ; but there may have been better reasons than are apparent for the strong and almost universal disapprobation with which the marriage was viewed by society.

PAGE **165,** l. 22. *else might I relate.* It is, I think, certain that in this letter, and in the last paragraph of the next (about the regatta), Johnson is writing in conscious parody of his own style.

PAGE **167,** l. 14. *talk not of the Punick war.* Charles James Fox once talked to Johnson about the Conspiracy of Catiline ; ' So I withdrew my attention, and thought about Tom Thumb '.

l. 21. Johnson's last letter to Mrs. Thrale ; to which she tells us that she ' returned an affectionate answer '.

PAGE **168,** l. 13. *the irremeable stream.* This is Virgil's *irremeabilis unda* (*Aeneid* vi. 425), the river of Hell which no man may recross.

PRINTED IN GREAT BRITAIN
AT THE UNIVERSITY PRESS, OXFORD
BY VIVIAN RIDLER
PRINTER TO THE UNIVERSITY